Ka•Gun•Da

George James Beck
Alaskan Pioneer Teacher, Missionary, Leader

Mary Giraudo Beck

Rocky Point Publishing
Ketchikan, Alaska

Also by Mary Giraudo Beck

Heroes and Heroines in Tlingit-Haida Legend

Shamans and Kushtakas
North Coast Tales of the Supernatural

Potlatch
Native Ceremony and Myth on the Northwest Coast

Text copyright 1999 by Mary Giraudo Beck

ISBN 0-9669478-1-9
Library of Congress Number: 98-83194

Cover Design: Steve Beck and Penny Laine Brunsdon

Rocky Point Publishing
2855 Tongass Avenue
Ketchikan, Alaska 99901

Would you call it a man's job to lead five hundred natives in their joys and sorrows, in politics, business, and religion: To stand watch in the wheel house all the way round the clock? To fight great waves, ice, rocks, fogs, darkness? To build coffins, dig graves, visit the sick, put down riots?

George James Beck's response to the question put by the Presbyterian Home Missions Board whether there was still a man's job in the Mission field.

Dedicated to those who accepted the challenge and
and to those who would give a life of service

ACKNOWLEDGMENTS

I would like to express appreciation to the following people for their help: Helen Finney, Nancy Ricketts, Betty Sterling, Bertha Karras, Frances Paul DeGermain, Wayne Duff, Steve Beck, Doug Beck, Katy Beck, Mary Jones, Reverend Robert Frye, and Elizabeth Richardson.

I am grateful too for assistance provided by the Sheldon Jackson College Museum and Library, the Sitka Museum and Historical Society, and the Ketchikan Library, Museum, and Tongass Historical Society.

A very special thank you goes to my husband George for supplying information from his memories of George James Beck, to Margot Miller for reading the manuscript and making helpful suggestions, to Richard Van Cleave for work on photographs, and to everyone at Angelo's Printing & Graphics.

CONTENTS

Aknowledgments 4

Introduction 7

Chapter I - New Horizons 10

Chapter II - Sitka Industrial School 22

Chapter III - Water Power 29

Chapter IV - Interim Superintendent 40

Chapter V - Sheldon Jackson School 48

Chapter VI - Kake and Hoonah 61

Chapter VII - Klukwan 74

Chapter VIII - Hoonah Again 88

Chapter IX - Ketchikan 109

Chapter X - Retirement 129

Appendix - S. Hall Young Article 137

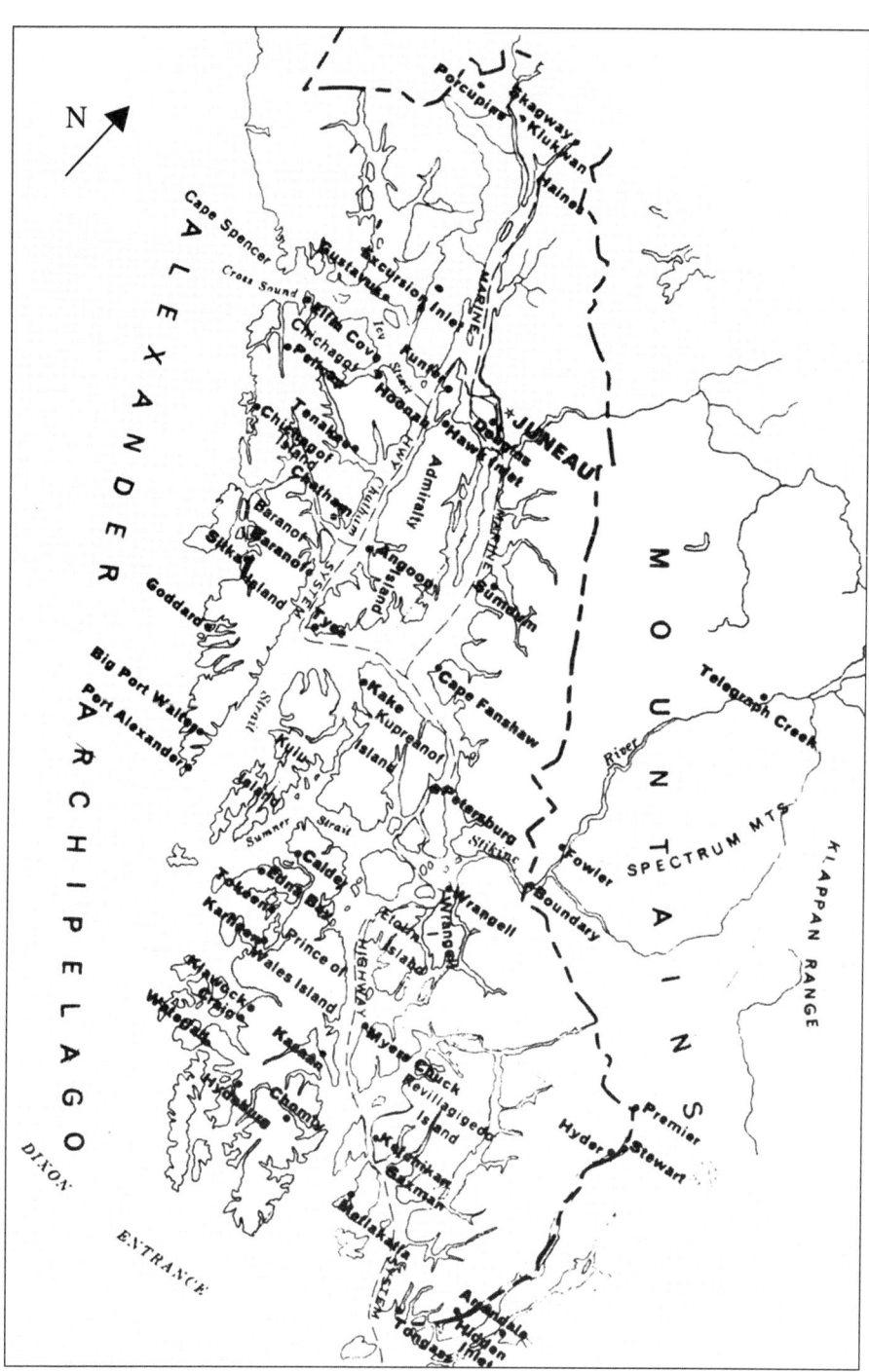

INTRODUCTION

When I first met George James Beck he was eighty years old, a retired minister wearing a three-piece navy serge suit, a hat, and a broad smile as he greeted us on the Alaska Steamship dock in Ketchikan. We had just disembarked from the S.S. Alaska; Bud was returning to his home with me, his recent bride. The suit and hat—and smile—I was later to learn, were his uniform and had been from the first day he began his Alaska mission. But along with the twinkle in his eye were a peace and assurance that suggested a life thoughtfully lived.

George Beck's missionary duty began in 1895 as the carpentry teacher at the Sitka Industrial Training School, now Sheldon Jackson College. He was not there long before he gained the title of Mission "Ka•gun•da," Tlingit for "light that comes from a fire." "The torch" would be an idiomatic translation, referring to the young man afire with enthusiasm, full of new ideas, and gifted in leadership. He had arrived at the school with his boundless enthusiasm and energy and a diversity of skills that would make him indispensable to the fledgling institution. But it was his dedication to his charges and understanding of their concerns that would account for his extraordinary influence in their lives.

As a lay missionary he had joined the force of Presbyterian missionaries who in the late 1870s had descended on Southeast Alaska in a whirlwind, determined to bring the natives to Jesus Christ through the Word and into the American mainstream through education. With unstoppable zeal and righteousness, they confronted the powerful, natives and whites alike, without fear of reprisal. And there was plenty of work for them to do, evil to overcome, native rights to be championed.

Hardly the picture of the zealous missionary, George came as a lanky, smiling young man ready for anything—"to serve," he had said. He had found his center early in life. He would need his determination and indomitable good nature to face what was before him. Nothing was going to be easy, not the actual physical work of life as a minister in the native villages; not the emotional pain at the loss of parishioners and immediate family. Fortunately, along with his down-to-earth charisma, he brought a hardy physique and optimistic outlook, skills of a journeyman carpenter, and a creative ability—a spark of his artist father's genius—to see and

Introduction

assess what was needed and to envision a way to provide it. These assets, along with the knowledge that "the Good Lord" was guiding his every step, would sustain him in heavy physical work as well as in personal loss.

When the missionaries who preceded him came with their fierce commitment to lead the natives to spiritual salvation, they quickly found themselves tending to their temporal needs as well. With the European influx came diseases that were decimating the natives and undesirable practices that were corrupting and abasing them. To tend the illness the Presbyterian Home Missions Board sent medical personnel, and to offset debilitating influences they sent teachers to educate the natives, train them in skills that could make them financially independent, and help them adjust to the foreign lifestyle. The missionaries hoped also that this training, along with their moral message, would encourage the natives to live law abiding lives in spite of the lawlessness that prevailed in the newly acquired territory, since for years after the purchase, the United States Congress had refused to enact laws necessary to establish order. For these Easterners, their duty was not only to lead the natives to spiritual salvation with the Protestant message, but also to imbue them with the Protestant work ethic as a means to their temporal salvation.

Inspired by the same missionary goals, George Beck threw himself into his teaching, training the boys in carpentry and working alongside them in repairing buildings and putting up new ones. When he saw the boys handsawing the huge amount of firewood needed to heat the buildings, he wondered whether the nearby river might be harnessed to power the saws. Once settled into his teaching, he pitched in with the boys to dig a ditch and build a flume to convey water from the river to the school and over a waterwheel they had put up for the purpose. Within the year the saws were mechanized. Later, with the help of the boys and some of the teachers, he built a more elaborate system that supplied the first lighting and electrical power to the school.

In addition to building and teaching, he held religious meetings at the school and in the town and tended the ill during influenza and small pox epidemics. His biggest asset was his exceptional rapport with the natives. Who else could be trusted to stake their ore-rich gold mine for them? The Presbyterian Home Missions recognized his gifts and insisted that he be ordained a minister although he had had no seminary training.

Introduction

After ordination in 1912 he was assigned first to Kake for four years, then Klukwan for less than a year, and finally to Hoonah for ten years, setting up elected councils of self-government in each place, encouraging agricultural projects, and building churches, manses, living quarters, and dams. Just as he began to feel he was making progress in one place, he was sent to another. Journals and letters show that during these years he spent a good part of his time visiting the ill and holding burial rites, which sometimes included building coffins and digging graves. He also took religious services to the hundreds of fishing and hunting camps of the area, manning the various boats of the "Presbyterian Navy" himself: the Star, the Lois, and the A.L. Lindsley. Finally he moved to Ketchikan in 1930, where he built a new church, gathered a large congregation, retired at 65 in 1936, and stayed until his death in 1962. During both world wars he took time from his Alaskan missionary work to serve as a civilian chaplain in the military. Every place he went he won the hearts of the people he was serving.

"I love my job," he was often heard to say. "I work for the Lord."

From the time of our first meeting on the dock, my admiration for this humble man continued to grow. Though I was late in knowing him, I was increasingly taken by his strong spirituality, laced with an unsuppressible cheerfulness. His was a way of life to strive for, a step toward peace and fulfillment.

NEW HORIZONS

The young man on the deck watched with fascination as the steamer wended its way through the hundred or more green islands at the entrance to Sitka, brilliant on their sparkling, white washed bases, like emeralds in diamond settings. Mt. Edgecumbe, an extinct volcano, rose to a height of 8,000 feet on an island at the entrance to the sound, while the peak of Verstovia rose above the semi-circle of lower mountains that formed a backdrop for the town. As they drew near to the dock in the harbor, he marveled at the many greens of the lush trees that grew down from the towering mountains to the gently sloped beach at the water's edge. His gaze followed the curve of the cove, taking in the rows of buildings that would be his new home.

George James Beck, a young man of boundless energy and enthusiasm and an indomitably cheerful nature, had been sent that summer of 1895 by the Presbyterian Home Mission in New York to teach carpentry at the Sitka Industrial Training School. He was about to join the other faculty and staff of the school at the start of its fifteenth year. What emotions were surging through him as he stood on the threshold of what would be a forty-year mission in Alaska, one can only imagine. Excitement, eagerness to get to work would have been one of them. For any New Yorker the isolation and strangeness of the place would have been overwhelming. But not for George Beck, who seemed not to know the meaning of fear. For him it would be another challenge. Nor on this day of the beginning of a new life, was there any way he could have suspected the deep, lasting influence he would have on the lives of the people of Southeast Alaska.

New Horizons

An idealistic young man, George had felt the urge to do something purposeful with his life. He had had intensive training in carpentry under his father's supervision. His father's name was also George, but the son had been given the identifying middle name of James when he was born on March 31, 1871. The family was living in New York City at the time of his birth, since the elder George Beck, a renowned sculptor and designer, had come from London to America to do work for the 1876 Centennial Exposition in Philadelphia. His wife Elizabeth joined him the following year and when the work for the fair was completed they decided to stay in America, where he continued to work at his various crafts for several New York companies, one of them Tiffany's. One of his more visible art works was the lions at the entrance to a New York City library. At some point later the Becks moved upstate to Eldridge, 90 miles north of New York City, where he was still able to pursue his career as an artist.

This talented and well educated parent, with his wife, taught George at home, but at the completion of eighth-grade level classes, he put his son to work on more practical matters—learning the woodworking trade. The elder Beck apprenticed the boy to himself, and by the age of sixteen George had built a twenty-one room Victorian house, complete with elaborate trim, thereby earning his journeyman papers. Before going to Sitka, he had also worked as a carpenter for five years and that with his intensive training would stand him in good stead at the Sitka Training School.

Having grown up in a family that was almost severely religious, where he had learned to read and write from the King James Bible, it was not surprising that he should present himself to the Alaska Presbyterian Mission Board in New York and ask "to be of service." On learning that George was a journeyman carpenter, the director immediately put him to work in the missions in New York, where the young carpenter proved himself skillful, innovative, and dependable and worked with an enthusiasm that inspired all around him. When an opening occurred for a carpentry instructor at the Sitka Training School in Alaska, the director offered him the position, which George quickly accepted, and dispatched him at once by train and boat to Sitka.

He was overwhelmed by the dark green of the still forested areas as the steamer pulled out of Puget Sound and, after touching port at Victoria, headed north through the Gulf of Georgia and into the Inside Passage, a long stretch of channels separated from the ocean by numerous islands. Only on Queen Charlotte and Milbanke Sounds and Dixon Entrance did they cross ocean waters en route to Juneau and Sitka. As the steamer journeyed on, he took in the beauty of the green islands, studded with trees growing out of the rock; the dark green, snow-capped mountains, and the quiet inlets. In the longest of the channels, Grenville, he watched as the mountains seemed to part like curtains to allow the steamer to make its way along the glassy smooth water.

The first stop in Alaska waters was at Metlakatla on Annette Island, where Father Duncan, originally an Episcopal minister, had led his Tsimpsian converts from Old Metlakatla in British Columbia after his break with the Church of England. By 1895, this village of 1500 had a sawmill, salmon cannery, blacksmith and shoe shops, and a general store, in all of which the workers were Tsimpsian.

The steamer stopped at each of the larger ports along the Inside Passage, giving George his first glimpse of places he would travel to often in his long career as teacher and eventually missionary. Then they were fishing villages, usually with a sawmill and a saltery or cannery. Ketchikan on Revillagigedo Island was the first stop, with its saltery, post office and Presbyterian and Episcopal missions for the two to three hundred natives. Most of this community was huddled along the bank and mouth of Ketchikan Creek. Next came Loring northeast of Ketchikan and also on Revilla Island, which had a salmon cannery, post office, and store for its population of both white and native people.

Wrangell, the following stop, had the largest native population, except for Sitka, in Southeast Alaska, commanding the entire trade of the Stikine River to the mainland. It had once been the main trading station of the Hudson Bay Company, under lease from the Russian-American Company, and later became the center of trade for the once rich Cassiar gold diggings in British Columbia. After the transfer of Alaska to the United States from Russia in 1867, it was used as a United States military post for several years until the troops were wholly withdrawn from Alaska. In 1895 the settlement had a sawmill, cannery, and several general stores.

On its way to and from Juneau the steamer passed the large islands of the Archipelago: Prince Of Wales (across from Ketchikan) and Kupreanof on the way north, and on its return southwestward to Admiralty, Chichagof,

New Horizons

and Baranof, all with mission settlements. Juneau, a trade and mining settlement as well as the center of the white population, sat at the base of a mountain three to four thousand feet high. Having a population of over a thousand in 1895, it had many frame buildings and public improvements, including water-works, electric lights, theaters, telephones, schools, and churches.

From Juneau the steamer went up to the head of Lynn Canal to the new settlements of Skagway and Dyea, points of departure for the Klondike and the Yukon in the interior, and then down to the mission at Haines on the east side of the canal. Quiet in 1895, these areas would boom in a few years with the 1898 Alaska Gold Rush. After a stop at Glacier Bay the steamer retraced its journey across Icy Strait to Hoonah on the north end of Chichagof Island, then south in Chatham Strait to Angoon and Killisnoo on Admiralty Island, and finally through Peril Strait between Chichagof and Baranof islands to Sitka. Since Sitka was the end of the route, passengers were given twenty-four hours to see the sights.

Sitka sat at the head of a harbor which was surrounded by hundreds of small islands. As the steamer wound through them the passengers looked with anticipation at the town ahead, no longer the Paris of the Pacific as it was called during Russian occupation, but still more built up than any of the other ports, save Juneau. Their attention quickly focused on the Graeco-Russian Cathedral of St. Michael, built originally in 1817 and rebuilt between 1846 and 1848. This latest building was noted for its Russian design, onion dome and bell chimes, and for the many ornate paintings and icons inside. Around the cathedral the town had spread out in a square, with the native settlement lying to the west somewhat up the hill and the training school east along the bay.

On disembarking, George was greeted by Reverend A. E. Austin and his wife, who would introduce him to the Sitka Training School. Reverend Austin, was superintendent of the school as well as pastor of the 400-member Presbyterian church in Sitka, and Mrs Austin was general matron of the school. Having held these positions for the fifteen years of its existence, they were considered the founders of the school, which officially dated from 1880, when their daughter Olinda Austin was appointed its first teacher. From the first, Reverend Austin insisted upon the importance of training the boys in trades and the girls in home duties, and in 1884 the

New Horizons

Sitka in 1890.

school was officially named the Sitka Industrial and Training School.

The group walked toward the campus, a semicircular row of buildings grouped around the bay. Passing the first building, they went to the next one, called the girls' dormitory building, although it also housed the administrative offices, classrooms, and dining area. Touring the inside, they stopped first at the primary grade classroom where Mrs. Saxman was reading to her primary grade pupils and after meeting her went on to the next room. There some students in the more advanced grades were working at their desks while Mrs. Heizer was drilling others in their times tables. After meeting Mrs. Heizer, Mr. Beck was taken to the kitchen and dining facilities in the same building, where he met Mrs. Coates and Mrs. Richardson, who were supervising the girls in fixing dinner.

Upstairs they toured the teachers' rooms and the girls' dormitory and then stopped to meet the girls' matron Miss Harriet Weaver and Mrs. Carter, who helped her oversee the care of that area. "Hundreds of demands are made on the poor, tired matron every day," said the May 1895 North Star of Miss Weaver, "and when night comes her cares do not end....She seems quite young, but just wait three or four years more and that peach bloom will be faded out of her cheeks." Certainly that still fresh peach bloom did not go unnoticed by the lively young man.

Reverend Austin led the way to the sewing department where Mrs. Wallace was teaching mending and sewing. Some girls were cutting out dresses, which they were learning to do without patterns, and others were working on intricate knitting and crocheting. From there the two men went over to the Sheppard building, where Mr. Beck would have his carpentry classes. There he was delivered to Mr. Frobese, a longtime teacher of painting and paper hanging, who would show him the other buildings. After viewing the industrial shops in the Sheppard building and stopping to talk with Mr. Solberg, who taught the boys shoe making and repair, they went on to the other buildings.

As they moved along, Mr. Beck noticed how the buildings appeared to be carved out of the backdrop of evergreens that seemed almost to envelope them. Walking along the shore he watched the water gently lap the beach while gulls hovered over the bay and an occasional raven swooped down to the ground. At a distance he could see some of the older boys cutting wood and younger ones hauling it up to the buildings. Maybe even

New Horizons

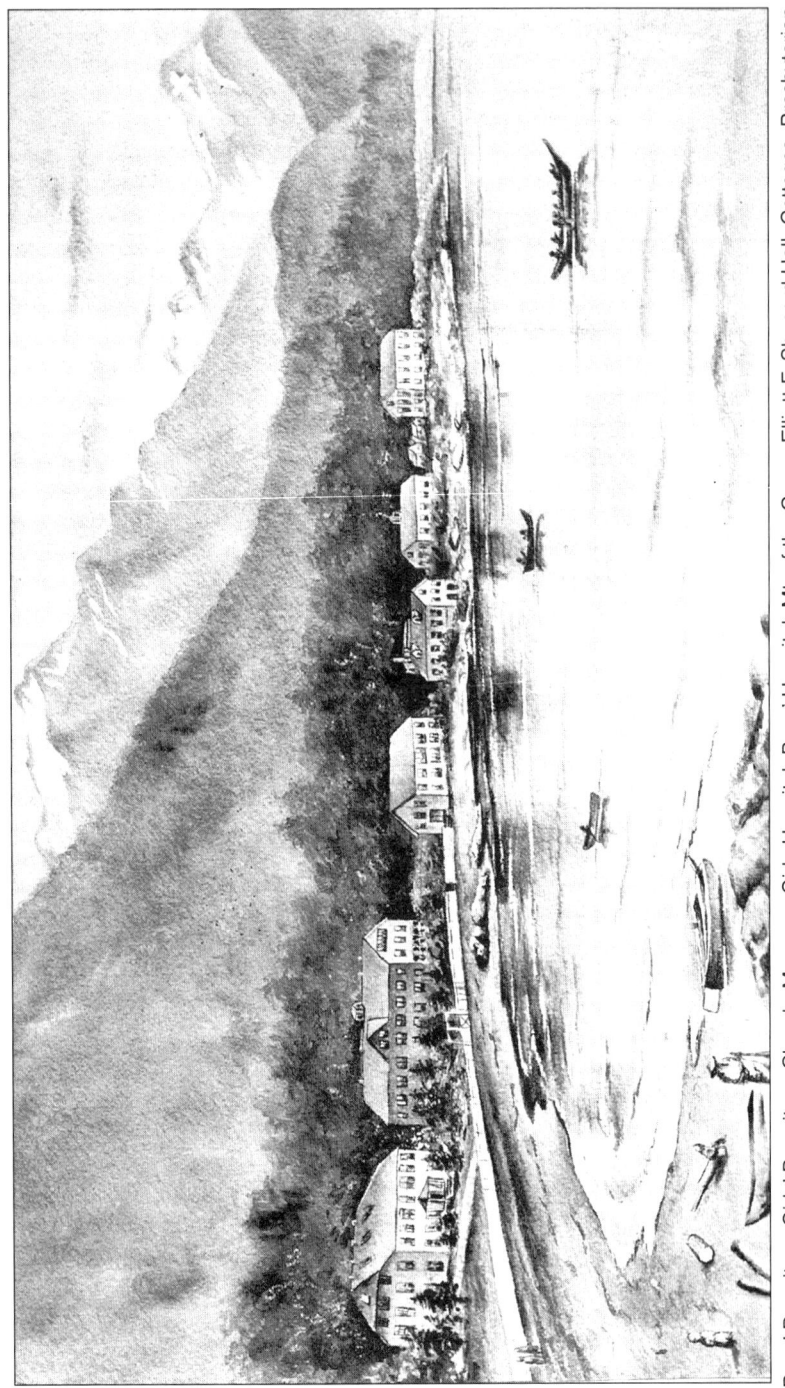

Boys' Dormitory, Girls' Dormitory, Church, Museum, Girls Hospital, Boys' Hospital, Mt. of the Cross, Elliott F. Shepard Hall, Cottages. Presbyterian Industrial School. Sitka, Alaska 1890. Ketchikam Museum 71.7.14.23.

New Horizons

at this moment, true son of a creative father, he wondered whether he could not devise a way to improve the efficiency of the wood cutting. After all the river was close by; perhaps that water power could be harnessed.

They went over to the last of the large buildings, which housed the hospital, where he met the physician and surgeon in charge, Dr. Wilbur, and his assistant, Miss Gibson, a trained nurse. Their patients included not only students but also townspeople in need of care. The doctor told the visitors that they lost very few children, although a young girl had died recently. The little one was still being grieved by the faculty and staff, who grew close to the children since through daily contact they got to know them well. In the rare times that the Dr. Wilbur was away from Sitka, the doctor on the naval ship filled in for him. Later through working together on the drill team, Dr. Wilbur and Mr. Beck were to become good friends.

Mr. Gamble, who was responsible for all the outdoor work, was checking on the hospital stove. He was a man of many other duties, whose versatility would have appealed to the broadly adept carpentry teacher. In addition to chores which few knew about, his work included tending the boiler that heated water for laundry and bathing, attending to the water works and the machinery in the laundry, and taking care of the team and stock. Beyond the hospital were the model cottages, where married native couples lived.

Woodshop after Waterwheel Installation.   Ketchikan Museums 71.7.14.156

New Horizons

All the buildings they had visited, along with the church and the parsonage, had been built by the students under the supervision and instruction of their teachers at the time. The museum, an octagonal, concrete structure—the first in Alaska—would be planned and contracted out that year. Mr. Frobese explained that students did all the manual labor in the school under the instruction and supervision of the teachers. Though these were skill-teaching activities, the older boys, who did the more difficult work, were paid.

As the men retraced their steps towards the girls' dormitory and teachers' rooms, Mr. Frobese explained at length the intricate system for the division of labor and training in each category. For work purposes, the girls were divided into three groups, eventually rotating in all of them to learn the skills for each. An older girl, who received a small compensation, headed each division. The kitchen and dining department prepared and served daily meals. Besides baking and cooking, the girls were taught the best way to handle and cook meat, fish and vegetables and to dry, smoke and store meat, fish, and berries. They also learned how to wait on and clear tables and to wash and put away dishes and silver.

The girls in the dormitory and sewing departments swept and scrubbed floors, dusted and arranged furniture, cleaned the lamps, and learned how to make beds and take care of clothes and bedding. In the sewing department the girls learned to cut out and make clothes; to alter, mend, and patch them; to knit and darn; and to use the sewing machines. The girls in the laundry department did the weekly washing and ironing of clothes and bedding.

The boys were divided primarily by age. The smaller ones cut and carried in fire wood, kept the grounds clean, and did other everyday chores. Mr. Beck would work more with the larger boys, who cut and rafted the logs for firewood, drew the seine when fishing, and did carpentry. Much of their work had to do with putting up the buildings, which included grading and ditching land, rafting logs and lumber, and getting rock for foundations and lumber for the building from the beach.

The young carpenter was especially interested in the process for getting the enormous amount of wood needed for heating the building. Mr. Frobese explained that since there were no roads or appliances for getting logs out of the woods, trees had to be selected near the shore so that, when cut, they

New Horizons

Boys Rafting Logs.

would fall into the water. The workers would then lash them together and, when the tide was right, float them toward the building site. After awhile all the trees close to Sitka had been cut, so that the boys had to go eight to ten miles for their annual supply of firewood, journeys that added to the fatigue and danger of the work. It spoke well for their seamanship that none of the boys were lost when occasional storms drove their boats ashore and scattered their rafts.

Mr. Beck was also amazed that the boys were practiced at using seines, which made it possible for them to take large loads of fish at once, a process he had not witnessed himself. Since fish was a major commodity of the territory, knowing about it provided a boy a way to make a good living. To be really skilled fishermen, the boys needed to learn the different species of fish, their names and habits, and their commercial value, as well as the various methods of catching and preparing them for market. They also needed to learn how to make and mend nets, handle and repair boats, and make sails and splice ropes. In addition the boys underwent periodic naval drill and received instruction on tides and compass use.

Mr. Beck was to teach classes in carpentry and to work with the boys in repairing and extending various buildings on campus. He had heard that Alaska natives were noted for skill in building canoes and in carving wood, stone, and metal, and he noticed that they very quickly became skillful in using tools. Among other things, they had been making furniture for their school as well as for other mission schools. Within a few months, the new woodworking instructor would be putting their skills to good use in building a large water wheel after digging a ditch and building a new flume in hopes of getting mechanical power to saw wood. But until he firmed up his plan he would start with boat building and repairs, skills some would continue to develop even after they left the school to become masters in their art.

As the two men neared the the laundry building, behind the girls' dormitory, they came upon the nearby bakery building, which had been left in ruins by a fire earlier in the year. Though that structure could not be saved, Mr. Frobese explained, the children and teachers had formed a bucket brigade to keep the fire from spreading to the other buildings. Shortly afterwards another fire had been discovered smoldering in the girls' dormitory, but it too had been put out by the boys and the Sitka Fire Brigade. Fires frequently originated where the stove pipe entered one of the flues, the wood outside the flue catching fire when the stove pipe slipped partially out of the flue. Fire was a real threat in those early years when the buildings were heated by wood and coal stoves and lighted by kerosene lamps.

Mr. Frobese continued the tour to the nearby laundry, which was in the care of Mrs. Matilda Paul, the only native teacher in the school. Besides her laundry duties, Mrs. Paul acted as translator between the Tlingit and nonnative people and frequently transcribed the business conducted. Mr. Beck and Mrs. Paul would be frequent co-workers in missionary work and become lifelong friends.

It was time for dinner when the two men had reached the girls' dormitory building, and they went right to the dining room. Though Mr. Beck had not been taken into the first building, Mr. Frobese explained that it housed the boys' dormitories and washrooms, as well as rooms for some of the staff.

They joined the other faculty in the dining room, where the students were in assigned places and the teachers and staff sat together at separate tables. Mr. Beck was asked about his trip and he picked up bits of news

New Horizons

about the school from the general conversation. He learned that various Presbyterian groups in the United States had sent boxes of used clothes for the children and other articles for the school. Most of the students' clothing came from donations. Though the winters were mild, Swan Lake did freeze over a few weeks in the winter and the children loved to skate on it. There was much talk of the presidential election to be held in October between McKinley and Bryan, decrying the fact the results would not reach them for three weeks after the elections, long after they were known to all of Europe.

The February 2, 1895, edition of the Sitka Alaskan announced the arrival of the new teacher: "Mr. George J. Beck of New York arrived on the last steamer to assume the position of chief carpenter in the Sitka Training School to succeed Mr. J. A. Shields, whose term has expired." The March edition of The North Star also announced that George J. Beck of New York had arrived February 1 and had immediately taken up his duties as teacher of carpentry in the Training School. "Mr. Beck comes to the work with a heart full of earnestness and consecration." His infectious cheerfulness and enthusiasm were to remain part of his character for life and to inspire the many people with whom he was to come into contact and influence.

SITKA INDUSTRIAL TRAINING SCHOOL

The Sitka Training School was only in its fifteenth year when George Beck arrived. An attempt at starting a school had been made in 1879 when Reverend John Brady, a Presbyterian minister, was sent to Sitka by the Home Mission at the urging of Sheldon Jackson, another Presbyterian who had distinguished himself as the Rocky Mountain Superintendent of Missions and had become interested in establishing missions in Alaska. Jackson had previously established a mission in Wrangell and persuaded Mrs. Amanda McFarland, who became the first American missionary in Alaska, to open a girls' school there. She was soon joined by the Reverend Dr. S. Hall Young to serve as the minister. In the first few years of his Wrangell ministry, Dr. Young laid the ground work for missions in Kake, Juneau, Haines, Killisnoo, and Hoonah.

At the urging of the native population and army personnel stationed in Sitka, Jackson persuaded the Board of Missions to authorize establishing a school there. With Miss Fannie Kellogg as teacher, the school opened in the spring of 1879 but was forced by a combination of circumstances to close in December. Fannie Kellogg married Reverend S. Hall Young, and Reverend John Brady resigned from his position with the Presbyterian Board of Missions to form the Sitka Trading Company, which operated a general store and a sawmill. In April of 1880 the school reopened as the Sitka Training School with Miss Olinda Austin as teacher, in a log building that had served as a Russian barracks and later as a US army barracks. So 1890 became the official first year of the school. That year Miss Austin and her mother joined her father, the Reverend A.E. Austin, who had come to Alaska the previous year as a lay missionary. She taught 103 students, mostly natives with a few whites and Russians. The following year Reverend Austin was appointed principal and Mrs. Austin, matron of girls. Then in 1884, in addition to these duties, Reverend Austin became minister of the Sitka Church, succeeding the Reverend G.W. Lyon, who had taken over after Reverend Brady resigned.

After the log building that housed the school burned in 1882, Jackson was able to raise $45,000 to rebuild the school plant. When the first permanent building—which was to become the boys' dormitory—was put up, the boys did all of the carpentry on it, and on all subsequent buildings,

Sitka Industrial School

under the instruction and supervision of John Walker, wood shop teacher at the time. For a water supply, iron pipes were laid for half a mile from the building to the Indian River.

During his lifetime Sheldon Jackson was one of the most influential of all the spokesmen on Alaska affairs. He made his first voyage to Alaska in 1877, when he helped organize the Wrangell mission, the first of his endeavors to bring Christianity to the natives. Though he never became a resident, he spoke to hundreds of groups, mostly in northeastern United States, asking for their aid against the influence of those whites who he believed were corrupting the native men with drink and casual use of young native women. In Washington he was well known among members of congress, being the close friend and fellow churchman of Benjamin Harrison, later president of the United States and author of the First Organic Act.

Early on, when Jackson noticed that the missions of the various church groups were competing for the same parishioners, he invited all of them to a meeting, where they agreed to parcel out the areas to the various denominations to avoid duplication of efforts. Then in 1884 with the passage of the First Organic Act, Congress appropriated $25,000 for the education of native and non-native children. The schools of the various church missions became "contract schools," supported jointly by the government and the various churches running them, until in 1883 government support of mission schools was withdrawn. Jackson was appointed general agent of education. As such he reported annually to the Federal Board of Education on the expenditure of funds and on the progress of the students. In these reports he gave statistics for the number of teachers and students and for the monthly student attendance.

In a letter dated March 12, 1883, Carrie Willard, wife of Eugene Willard, the missionary at Haines, described the single building of the Sitka Training School, the building still standing in 1895 and known as the boys' dormitory: "The two-story mission building, one hundred feet front and fifty feet deep, stands on an eminence which slopes gently to the beach just where the avenue, following the waterline, enters the green wood, and a branch road to the left winds up around the house and through the brush wood farm at its rear. The house is frame, plain and substantially built, containing, besides the teachers' apartments and those intended for the

Sitka Industrial School

home of the children, a large room for the accommodation of the day school, which is also used for Sabbath services. There are now forty-six boys in the home, whose ages range from eight to seventeen years. Most of them are quick to learn and show an aptness for trades." By 1895 the school rooms and some teachers' quarters were housed in the girls' dormitory building.

The annual government reports of Sheldon Jackson as Agent of Education give a good idea of the working of the school in these early years, while the North Star, the school publication, reveals every day happenings among the students and teachers.

Jackson's report to the Federal Board of Education for 1884 listed himself as superintendent of the Sitka Training School from July 1884 until March 1885, when he was replaced by A.J. Davis until June, and finally by William A. Kelly for the remainder of the year. The reverend Alonzo E. Austin was assistant superintendent and chaplain. John Walker, a United States Indian who received industrial training at an Indian trade school, was industrial teacher from July to March, during which time he supervised the students in the construction of many of the first campus buildings. He was succeeded by Thomas Keaton from March to June. Other faculty included Mrs. Austin, matron boys' department; Mrs. A. R. McFarland, originally with the girls' school in Wrangell, matron girls' department; Miss Kate Ranking, sewing; Miss Margaret Dauphin, kitchen and laundry; Mrs. R. A. Koalas, school room; W.D. McCleod, machinist; David Jackson, boot and shoe department; Mr. Cryogen, watchman; and Sergeant Myers USN, volunteer drill master.

Statistics for the 1884-85 school year showed an enrollment of 137 students, 47 boys and 90 girls. The average age for the boys was 14 years and for girls was 10 1/2. There were three deaths and one marriage. One boy and one girl had died of consumption and one girl of pneumonia. The boy's death was the first in the boys' department in the five-year history of the school, remarkable in light of the dangerous way the boys obtained firewood. There is no mentioned of who was married.

In 1884 the school was given the official name of the Sitka Industrial and Training School, later familiarly shortened to Sitka Training School. In 1886 The North Star was begun, with Sheldon Jackson as editor and the Rev. A.E. Austin and Dr. B.K. Wilbur as associate editors.

Sitka Industrial School

Jackson's education report of 1888 mentioned that a student band had been organized after the school had received a donation of 21 brass instruments. A military company of 35 students had also been formed, for which guns had been loaned by the governor. The following year Superintendent Kelly reported that older children who had been with the school several years had developed a sense of personal responsibility, self-respect, and self-reliance.

The first mention of livestock came with an announcement in the January 1890 North Star of the acquisition of a team of horses for the school. Money for the horses, Corona and Ancon, had been contributed by passengers aboard the ships Corona and Ancon, which had stopped at the port of Sitka August 20, 1889. "Upon inquiring as to the amount needed for a team of horses," reported the North Star, "we modestly suggested that it would take about $300. In less than 15 minutes the generous hearted, enthusiastic audience contributed the sum of $395," enabling the purchase of the horses and leaving $72 for feed and $30 for harnesses.

Student Edward Marsden, a Tsimpsian who was later to become the first Alaska Native protestant minister, described the school's daily routine in the March 1890 North Star. A bell rang at six o'clock a.m. to waken all teachers and students. Lamps were lighted by the Sergeants and "Get up!" sounded from the boys' dormitories. Once everyone was dressed, the wash rooms were opened and the boys and girls washed their faces and combed their hair and got ready for the day. Those who helped prepare and distribute food, however, were wakened at four-thirty or five.

As early as 1893 disapproval of the wood-stove heating system was sounded. In the 1893 government report Mr. Kelly wrote that he did not approve of the method of heating used in the school—a stove in every building—feeling it was "unsafe, unsatisfactory, and inadequate." Periodic fires in the buildings supported his point. He also commented on the success of the model homes for married couples who had attended the school. That year's report included the name of Miss Harriet Weaver as one of the new teachers. George J. Beck's arrival was announced in the 1895 report.

Articles from various 1895 issues of the North Star, edited at that time by Superintendent U. P. Skull, Principal A.E. Austin, and Dr. B.K. Wilbur, reveal much that went on during that year. The February issue reported that there were 151 native boys and girls in attendance, "all fed, clothed,

Sitka Industrial School

housed and taught without any cost to them. Each is taught the rudiments of an English education and also some industry. The boys are to work in the carpenter shop, shoe shop, steam laundry, and bakery, while the girls learn sewing, knitting, cooking, baking, and general housework."

"The boys that go out from the school command good wages and have little trouble finding employment, especially during the summer season. Their habits of industry and ability to talk English, together with their ability to do different kinds of work, insure them profitable employment.

"The girls are less fortunate in finding employment, as they are limited to housework, sewing, washing, etc. The most desirable policy is for them to marry honorable young men of their own people and to establish homes. The model cottages in connection with the school, with their pure home life, fully demonstrate the feasibility of the plan." A later issue during the summer remarked that the native people of Southeast Alaska were lively, cheerful and joyous, and teachers mentioned in their reports to the US Bureau of Education that they were industrious, hard working, and self-supporting, working long days fishing and hunting and preserving foods. Most of the pupils were Tlingit from Southeast Alaska, but there was one Aleut and one Eskimo at that time.

Rudolph Walton, a former mission boy, advertised his silver and gold workshop in the April 1895 North Star. He had on hand silver and gold rings, bracelets, napkin rings, spoons, tongs, and ladles, and would also make similar items to order. The same paper mentioned that Mr. Beck was hard at work remodeling the building known as the girls' hospital for a parsonage to be occupied by the Reverend and Mrs. A.E. Austin.

In April came an exciting announcement: "Plans, specifications, and detailed drawings have been submitted for the new Sheldon Jackson Museum, for which Reverend Jackson, concerned about the safety and care of the many precious artifacts, donated the funds himself. The materials to be used in construction will be gotten out at once at Mr. J. G. Brady's saw mill." The museum was to have concrete walls, and would be octagonal in shape. By July a brief article mentioned that under the management of Dr. Jackson and Boston architect Mr. John Smith, the walls of the new museum were rising "like those of ancient Carthage under the direction of Queen Dido."

Another article described the eight model cottages, which had been built

Sitka Industrial School

and occupied during the fifteen years of the school's existence, as being two-story frame houses with kitchen and dining and sitting rooms downstairs and two bedrooms upstairs. They were occupied by former students and their wives and children. Built at the cost of $400 each, they had been sold to the natives on the installment plan without interest. "Most of these young people are industrious, earnest Christians, self-supporting and self-respecting," Dr. Wilbur, said.

A picture of a somewhat discouraged Dr. Wilbur emerges from his comments in the April paper on the nature of his work: "One of our wards recently had three patients, all consumptives in advanced stages, all expecting the white doctor to cure them at once, all coughing and growing despondent. It was a real trial to make the rounds there, and so much of our work is of this deep-seated chronic character. It requires much patience, cheerfulness and hope, together with great faith in God, to keep from the slough of despond ourselves." The December 1895 issue gave a brief account of the Sitka Mission Hospital activity for the year. Eighty-six people were treated, 69 of them new patients, and averaged over 10 days' board. Eight patients died, nine were unimproved, 35 improved, and 52 were cured. Illnesses included arthritis, bronchitis, buboe, dysentery, dysmenorrhoea, fractures and lacerations, and tuberculosis, to name but a few. A comment on a later page reported that in November an operation on the skull was performed. The same issue mentioned that while Dr. Wilbur was in Philadelphia, patients at the hospital had been being treated by Dr. Adrian Alfred of the US Pinta.

A few months later Dr. Wilbur had a more cheerful article about a sailing and hiking trip to Mt. Edgecumbe on an island about ten miles from the school. Despite the wind and rain that developed, the five staff members and their native guides had an invigorating and delightful time. The trip usually entailed an overnight stay, which the more adventurous generally spent in the crater of the volcano. However, Dr. Wilbur exhorted his readers always to heed the advice of the natives on the weather, since his guides, who had advised against the trip beforehand, had been proven right in foreseeing the storm.

The August North Star announced the opening of a mission school for the Cape Fox and Tongass natives on a site at the lower end of Tongass Narrows, eighteen years after two missionaries, S.A. Saxman and Louis

Sitka Industrial School

Paul, and Edgar, a native guide, were drowned in an attempt to establish a school and mission work there in the winter of 1886-7. Mr. Paul was the husband of Matilda Paul, who moved from Wrangell to the Sitka Training School after his death.

Several news tidbits were reported in subsequent issues of the paper. The Sheldon Jackson museum was near completion and the architect, John J. Smith, and his wife had returned to the States. Distinguished visitors to Sitka during the summer had included Lieutenant General Schofield, head of the federal army next in command to the President of the United States; Vice-president of the United States Stevenson, and Rear Admiral Walker. Miss Hattie Weaver, girls' matron, was on an outing with twenty of the older girls to enjoy the mineral water and sulfur baths of the Hot Springs. Sitka Bay was literally alive with herring at the time. One of the mission boys was able to get a barrel of them in less than two hours by drawing a long, sharp-toothed rake through a school of the small fish and impaling them on its teeth. "Mr. George J. Beck conducts a Sabbath school in the Indian village every Sabbath afternoon for those who cannot attend Sabbath school at the mission. It has met with great success." Mrs. Paul was accompanying him both as a missionary and a translator.

By this time a Presbyterian mission had been established at Saxman, a native village near Ketchikan, under the supervision of Reverend Edward Marsden. Genevieve Bayberry reported in her early history of Sheldon Jackson School: "In 1895 Edward Marsden, graduate of the Sitka school, was ordained to the ministry, the first Protestant Alaskan Indian to attain this honor. Under the sponsorship of Dr. Jackson, he had been graduated from Marietta College. He received his degree in theology from Lane Theological Seminary and, in 1898, established a Presbyterian Mission at Saxman. His purchase of a 36-foot steam launch to be used in mission work was the first Presbyterian boat to ply southeastern Alaska waters and was the beginning of the several boats since used in the work, and that have been called the 'Presbyterian Navy." Years later as an ordained minister, Mr. Beck would man the Lois, a Presbyterian vessel that he used to take the Word to the natives at their fishing camps. His beloved Lois would also be the occasion of a harrowing, life-threatening event for him.

WATER POWER

As his first year progressed, Mr. Beck was seen often in the company of Hattie Weaver, but, as he told his family much later, always well chaperoned by flocks of students. By the completion of his first year at the training school in early 1896, George Beck had settled in as carpenter and lay missionary, pitching in with his students wherever needed and continuing his mission meetings in the village.

The museum building was well under way. The January 1896 North Star gave a detailed description of its progress and of the care of the collection of artifacts, which had been garnered primarily by the Society of Alaskan Natural History and Ethnology, organized in October of 1887. "The society succeeded in gathering a valuable collection of Alaskan curios and skins, specimens of Eskimo and Indian handiwork, all sorts of ivory carvings . . . representative curios of all parts of Alaska. For several years this accruing collection has been kept in a small wooden house much too small to serve as a museum. . . Dr. Jackson has solved the problem, and to his generosity the society is indebted for a large and commodious structure, ...being built of concrete...with concrete floors..and consequently fireproof. The interior shows a diameter of 62 feet and a height in proportion. The hip roof is capped with an observatory and flag mast, and the whole cost of erection has been $5,000."

Matilda Paul was featured in the March North Star with a front page picture of her and her children and a lengthy article on her childhood and marriage. Tillie was born in Wrangell and attended Mrs. McFarland's school, where she learned impeccable English. With her natural ability in her native Tlingit, by the age of fifteen she became the official missionary interpreter. When she married Louis

Matilda Paul and son William

Water Power

Paul, the two dedicated their lives to missionary work. Upon the death of her husband, she went to the Sitka Training school, where she also served as interpreter. The same article reported that the village on Tongass Narrows where the school for the Cape Fox and Tongass would be located had been named Saxman, after one of the men who drowned along with her husband in the winter of 1886-87 while searching for a suitable location for a school and mission. The only native worker in the school, Mrs. Paul had been connected with various departments for several years and was at that time in charge of the steam laundry.

Then came an unexpected announcement in the September 1896 North Star. "At the mission parsonage August 4, 1896, Mr. George J. Beck and Miss Hattie Weaver were united in marriage by Reverend A. E. Austin. Mr. Beck is in charge of carpentry in the Training School and Miss Weaver was, during the last three years, matron of girls. The North Star wishes the newly wedded pair a prosperous voyage on life's tempestuous sea."

The Sitka Alaskan gave a more romantic report: "Mr. George Beck and Miss Hattie Weaver were joined together in the bonds of holy matrimony at the Mission parsonage Sunday by the Reverend A.E.Austin. It was a very quiet wedding and later the newly married couple in an independent way, scorning the steam boat conveyance within the iron walls and bound to stop at every calling place of the vessel, which sometimes makes a port long after sundown, rendering the time that should be devoted to sleep or at least to rest, and almost unbearable by the grunt and roll of a donkey engine unloading freight, we say scorning these means of travel they set forth on their honeymoon in a sail boat and free as the winds of Heaven they can roam from isle to isle and pitch their tent where seems best, far from the madding crowd, untrammeled by conventionalities and with all the liberty of the birds, to those 'souls with but a single thought , those hearts that beat as one,' the world of love will be the sweetest world of all."

Upon their return, work went on as usual for the newlyweds. The October issue of the North Star commented, "The machinery in the shop is now running by water power. Mr. Beck, the carpenter, has shown no little enterprise in opening the old flume leading from the Indian River and constructing a water wheel. It looks quite business-like in the shop when the machinery begins to hum. The lathe, the circular saw, the former, and others will be made to attach and run by the water wheel."

Water Power

Early on, Mr. Beck's leadership ability and personal magnetism was making itself felt. He worked hard and people were drawn by his enthusiasm and energetic manner. They admired him for his ability to do so many different things. No work was beneath him. When digging the ditches needed for the flow of water driving the pelton wheel or for the piped water that would bring electricity to the school, Mr. Beck pitched in with the boys. But most of all they could sense his acceptance of them as people and it did not take him long to win them over. They wanted him to help them. They wanted to be like him. They went to him for advice. This rapport with the natives was to stand him in good stead for his whole missionary life.

An issue of the North Star in the previous July had mentioned that Sitka tourists were interested in visiting the school and were impressed with the work being done in the various departments and with the natives in the way of practical education. "Many say they have heard that it is useless to try to do anything for the natives and that the money put into educational work in Alaska is thrown away. It is gratifying to see that when they have looked upon the work that is being done here, they discover that there must be some motives prompting these disparaging remarks."

This statement touched upon the conflict that existed between some of the white people of Sitka, several of them government appointees in positions of power, which dated at least as early as the first $25,000 given by Congress in 1884 to fund the education of children in Alaska regardless of race. Many felt the white children were being neglected, since the greatest number of students were natives, who also attended the religious missions schools. The fact that Sheldon Jackson, a staunch, politically powerful Presbyterian, was the Agent for Education in Alaska added to their fears. Those who objected to government funding of the missions eventually won out when Congress put an end to it in 1893. But this action did not end the hostility toward the mission schools. The loss of government funding affected all the mission schools, causing some to have to close.

The same North Star article showed a drop in enrollment at the training school in 1896, although the salaries of five teachers there were paid by the government. "There are at present about ninety boys and girls in the school. The plant will accommodate many more, but on account of financial depression the number has been limited to save expenses. . . . The Educational work of the Board is directly committeed to the Woman's Executive Committee ...organized in 1878 and now supporting 114 schools in the U.S. with 319 teachers and 9,466 pupils." This issue also expressed gratitude for donations of clothing from various religious school groups and by Ladies' Home Missionary societies.

According to the 1896 Education Report, the girls' hospital was moved to the enlarged upper floor of the building that housed the boys' hospital, the project the North Star had earlier reported was being done by Mr. Beck and his boys, and the combined unit became open to natives from any part of Alaska. The same report also announced that as a matter of preservation, the Society of Alaskan Natural History and Ethnology had begun to put the Tlingit language into writing, with the help of Mrs. Paul and Miss Willard [of Haines], both of whom spoke Tlingit. The Society was organized and incorporated in the winter of 1887-88 to collect specimens of artifacts and ethnology of Alaska.

Mr. Gamble's garden was commented on at length in that year's report. As gardener and general worker, Mr. Gamble had three medium-sized plats of arable land. One garden, which had been cultivated for several years, produced lettuce, beets, peas, and onions. Of the two newer gardens, one was planted in potatoes and the other in turnips. Cereals, for lack of warmth, would not ripen. Currants, raspberries, rhubarb, cauliflower and celery grew easily.

All the buildings had been built by boys apprenticed to the building trade. Indoor carpentry work included the making of clothes presses, screens, chests, curtain poles, and picture frames. Sail making and boat building were also done in carpentry class.

But it was not all work and no play at the Sitka Training School. Not many schools anywhere had organized sports and neither did Sitka Training School, but the students did play baseball, townball, hide-and-seek,coating, skating, marbles, and soldiers, and practiced the bow and arrow. Quieter activities included playing checkers, reading, and playing mouth organs, even violins.

If dwindling funds concerned the teachers and staff, they did not seem to affect the performance of the students. The October North Star found that "The boys and girls in the Training School are showing more eagerness and enthusiasm in their books and studies than they have ever shown

Water Power

before. The return of Miss Flora Campbell and the visits of Edward Marsden, Miss Wells, and other natives who have acquired a liberal education in the States have furnished proof to these boys and girls of the refining and elevating influence of higher education and fired them with zeal and determination."

A later comment revealed that a number of boys and girls had been sent east to school, among them "our only Eskimo, little Healy Wolfe. This diminutive half-blood Eskimo of eleven years is as bright and capable as the average white boy, if indeed not above the average, and is sure to make his mark if he has the opportunity. We were loath to give him up and yet we are glad that he can have the privilege of better facilities than the schools of Alaska can afford." As in many other instances, the staff and teachers here showed their regard and concern for their charges. An earlier issue of the paper had printed the poem of the then nine-year-old boy.

> THE MOLE
> The mole is a very curious animal.
> The mole is about the size of a rat.
> It is with a dark skin.
> The fur standing straight from its body.
> The legs of the mole is short, and it can not rise from the ground.
> The forelegs are large, and short, and strong.
> The mole is a good worker, and he makes a nest of dried grass.
> The mole makes tunnels around its nest.
> He digs down into the ground for his food.
> When he digs he throws the dirt back.
> The mole has eyes but we can not see them because they are far down his fur.
> He has good hearing and a good smelling.

The January 1897 North Star featured a picture and article on the Training School shoe shop. That department was seen as important in teaching the boys a useful trade and also as an economic measure, since all the shoes for the hundred or more pupils were made and repaired there. The shop also did a certain amount of custom work, which brought in about forty or fifty dollars a quarter. But there was concern about the future em-

Water Power

ployability of the boys. After graduation the students were often unable to find employment in their field, as there were no shops to hire them. "At present there is not a demand for more than two dozen good shoemakers in all of Alaska, while double that number of carpenters could easily do all the work that is required in that line. When the boys go out from the training school with a trade fairly mastered, they often find more profitable employment in the mines, sawmills, and canneries, and do not follow their trade." But the staff felt that each pupil should have a trade in case a demand did arise for his services. They also felt that training in a trade cultivated steady habits of industry in the boys.

Several news items told of events taking place in 1897 and 1898. The January 16, 1897, Alaskan reported: "Mr. George Beck, the Mission carpenter, went to Saxman on the boat to investigate its needs from a missionary point of view and may conclude to engage in missionary work there." And a week later: "Mr. Beck returned from Saxman on the Topeka. He reports a population of about 140 in that new native village and is thinking seriously of going there in the coming spring to engage in missionary work." That plan would have been thwarted by the appointment of Reverend Marsden to the post in 1898. But already Mr. Beck's zeal to be a full-fledged missionary was coming to light, though that desire would not be realized for more than ten years.

Agricultural projects were a vital concern to the missionaries, who felt the Natives' living conditions would be improved if they could raise some of their own food. Mr. Gamble's garden at the school was an experiment in this direction. Such experiments were evidently taking place elsewhere, as the March 1897 paper commented on some rutabagas a Mr. Hubbard had brought to the school from his garden in Killisnoo. The visitor explained that he and a Mr. Baker had diked about eighty acres of tide land south of Killisnoo to keep out the sea water and continued to till the ground, making it rich and productive and in need of no irrigating or fertilizing.

In August 1898 the Alaskan mentioned that Mr. and Mrs. George Beck had moved into new quarters over the store house which had been slightly remodeled and enlarged. "The Mission 'Ka.gun.da,' as the Natives call Mr. Beck, seems very happy." This is the only reference found to the boys' endearing name for their teacher, which has been translated as "a light from a fire," or a torch.

Water Power

At the beginning of 1900, he was designated to take the census of the villages of Southeast Alaska. Given that most of the villages had to be reached by small boat, this was a more daunting experience than it appeared to be. According to the January Alaskan, "George J. Beck and William Wells from the Presbyterian Mission left on the Cottage City and will take the census at Killisnoo, Hoonah, and other villages." Then in a later issue: "After an absence of nearly three weeks, George J. Beck has returned from his census-taking trip. He came from Hoonah in a small rowboat and reports he had a very rough trip." As he told the family much later, he set out from Hoonah with some dependable native boatmen in an open boat rowing to the various villages, putting up a square sail when the wind permitted. Along with a tent for pitching on land each night, they had packed blankets and extra clothing, which they kept carefully covered to keep them dry. Since much of the travel was done in winter, it was cold and there were no berries or edible plants, but they were able to supplement their dried supplies with fresh fish and seafood and an occasional deer.

By 1901, Mr. Beck and his students were at work building a new flume that would power a larger water wheel to generate power for the larger tools, primarily the large saw that cut firewood for all the buildings. Ac-

Overhead Flume to Waterwheel.

Water Power

cording to the July 27 North Star, "The flume that is being built near the Mission is to enlarge the power at the carpenter shop. It will be utilized in running the lathe, saw, and other pieces of machinery, and if sufficient to saw logs, it will be used in that way."

By the following month, they were working on the water wheel (August North Star): "Mr. Beck is working hard to install the new 16-foot water wheel at the Mission carpenter shop. The old flume has been enlarged and carried over the road and it does not leak either. The improvements are expected to develop enough power to saw all the firewood required for the Mission." This understated description leaves much to imagination. In actuality, the new flume started a mile or more up the grade near the river on a trestle supported by posts and hovering sixteen feet above the road so that when the water reached the sixteen-foot water wheel, it could pour down over the wheel. The center shaft of the water wheel extended into the shop building where it was connected by belts and pulleys to the various tools. The outside saw used for cutting logs was linked

Mr. Beck with Waterwheel Powered Drag Saw.   Ketchikam Museums 71.7.14.148.

Water Power

Waterwheel. Sitka Museum PH1700.

Water Power

Waterwheel Powered Pulleys.   Sitka Museum PH1701.

to the same shaft and powered by the water wheel.

Mr. Beck had come up with the idea for this project and had designed it himself, with little or no previous experience with that type of work. He could do anything, figuring out how something should be done as the occasion demanded and then becoming adept at doing it. Some of his success with this project was due to having perfected the tools of his trade under a strict indentured apprenticeship, which surely had included some surveying and basic practical engineering and required an ability to improvise. But most of his success was due to his own enterprise and creativity, along with a penchant for challenging the impossible.

The automating process of the waterwheel was still mechanical, since electric power was not yet available in Alaska, although Juneau did have some electric lighting. An 1898 article in the Alaskan bewailed the lack of electricity and water power in Sitka.

"Sitka needs a system of water works and an electric light plant. They can be put in at a cost of about $25,000. Water at present is brought from the Indian River, which is a mile and a half from town. Kerosene oil is

Water Power

used by our citizens for illuminating purposes. Insurance is almost unknown in Alaska and most of our homes are uninsured. The United States government would derive the greatest benefit from the establishment of water works and electric light. Here are located the US penitentiary, custom house, Marine barracks, and other public buildings." In addition to the inconvenience caused by the lack of electricity, the danger of lighting with kerosene was decried.

Jackson's 1899-1900 report for the Sitka Training School showed an enrollment of 147 boarding pupils and four day pupils; nine teachers, two of whom were Native; salaries and expenses totaling $15,693.32; $297.10 was taken in from tuition. That year Mr. William A. Kelly was still superintendent, assisted by Dean W. Richards. Misses Susan Davis, Sadie Martindale, Anna M. Sheets, Lucile Owen, and Frances Willard (native) had replaced the other matrons while John E. Gamble and Howard George (native) were teachers. Mrs. Matilda Paul (native), was the interpreter while and Dr. B.K. Wilbur and Miss Esther Gibson had an assistant nurse, Miss Anna Hinds (native). Reverend S. Hall Young D.D., was on furlough. Although he was not listed, George J. Beck was teaching carpentry and industrial subjects at that time.

For some reason, Mrs. E. C. Heizer and Mrs. Selina Gamble were not listed either, but both gave reports on their classes. Selina Gamble, who had the lower three grades, reported that some of her students had moved out of their primers and had been put into higher grades. She had been teaching them several songs, since the Native children enjoyed music and liked to sing. Mrs. Heizer, who taught the higher three grades, was in her seventh year of teaching at the school. "Many of the pupils have gone out from us during this time and started life alone. To learn to plan for themselves is the hardest lesson for them, but this they can learn only by experience. A number of the boys are working at the mines in Juneau and Douglas Island. One is in a sawmill in Sitka. He has built a very nice home in the Cottage settlement. They frequently call to see us and love their alma mater."

INTERIM SUPERINTENDENT

Sheldon Jackson's reports continue to give information about the Sitka Training School in those early years. None of the teachers listed in the 1900-1901 report are new, but this time Mr. Beck was listed as teaching carpentering, furniture making, and boat building, and Mrs. E.C. Heizer and Mrs. Selina Gamble were included. Enrollment remained at 151.

Sickness besieged Southeast Alaska and especially Sitka Training School during this time. But some good news came shortly afterwards with the discovery of a gold mine by some former students on Chichagof Island a few miles from Sitka on nearby Baranof.

In the government reports, both Mrs. Heizer and Mrs. Gamble bemoaned the toll that sickness, especially the outbreak of smallpox, took on attendance and performance at the training school. And both public schools were closed for a period of time because of smallpox. The hospital reported that smallpox was epidemic and "teachers acted heroically in caring for the sufferers."

Among the heroic teachers was George J. Beck, who, though he had a small daughter at home, ministered physically and spiritually to the smallpox sufferers. Mr. Beck told his family later that he went each afternoon to visit the smallpox patients who had been isolated on Japonski Island. Conditions were terrible for the ill, who lay crowded in shacks with hardly the bare necessities. To avoid infecting himself or spreading the disease to others, he would stop first at a shack on the island to put on special clothing for his visits, which he would then change out of when he was returning to Sitka. These trips helped lift the morale of the patients, who for sanitary precautions were deprived of visits from families and friends, and he was able to give them some physical and spiritual comfort. He helped care for the sick, bury the dead, and disinfect furnishings. He was also able to convey messages from families and friends and to report to them on the condition of patients. To those who thought he was exposing his family and associates with unwarranted risk, he said merely, "Whatever is in the Lord's plan is all right with me." Nobody at home came down with smallpox.

Woodcutting at the Sitka Training School was an unending activity, as the buildings were heated by coal and wood. The June 1, 1901, paper re-

Interm Superintendent

ported that Mr. George Beck left with twelve boys from the mission to cut wood for the winter, accompanied by Mrs. Beck. The group would have gone to a distant spot to fell trees and then raft them to Sitka, where they would be cut up for firewood.

Having been at the training school for six years by 1901, Mr. Beck had built up a certain trust with the boys, who often came to him for advice or help once they had left the school and started lives of their own. One big moment of trust between him and the boys had to do with what eventually became known as the Chichagof Mine. Since the 1898 Gold Rush in Alaska, there was much searching for gold deposits in the area, and many claims had been staked on Chichagof and Baranof Islands. Two former students had been out fishing with five other men in a boat, which stopped off in Flag Bay on Chichagof for all on board to walk a bit and get some fresh water. When the two former students were kneeling by the stream and had started drinking, they noticed gold in one of the many pieces of quartz lying in the bed of the stream. Picking one up to examine it more closely, they found that the ore had much more free gold than usual. The two returned to the boat but kept quiet about their find. At a later time they went back alone to the same spot and panned as much gold as they could to take back with them for testing in Sitka. At the same time they traced the gold to what appeared to be its source.

Assayers in Sitka recognized the ore as having a very high yield of gold, but only after mining was well under way did they realize how high. On the market the ore of the Chichagof mine (known also as the DeGroff mine after the man who had grubstaked them) netted $1200 per ton of ore compared with the $75-per-ton yield of the Douglas Treadwell mine. The original samples that the two men brought for testing netted $1,350 from Tacoma Smelters, who received a good percentage of that for their work.

With sure knowledge of their good fortune, the men approached Mr. Beck, their former teacher, whom they knew they could trust with their precious secret. They asked if he would file the claim for them, offering him a fourth of the profits for his efforts. The two discoverers each would maintain a fourth interest and the remaining fourth would go to the person who would provide them with the necessary groceries and supplies.

When Alaska attained its first civil government with the Organic Act of 1884, the miners' code continued to operate for staking mine claims

Interm Superintendent

because the Act was unclear in regard to the ownership of land. But even under the miner's code, Alaska natives, who lacked citizenship, were unable to stake their own claims. White men could easily jump their claims and win any litigation that might follow. Their best option was to have a white man stake the claim for them for a percentage of the value of the mine.

Mr. Beck did not want to get involved with any financial undertaking, fearing it would distract him from the job he came to do. Besides, he wanted the natives to feel that anything he did for them had no cost attached. Money was to play no part in the help he offered them. But he did agree to go with them to survey and stake out the claim properly.

In such a small community it was impossible to keep the transaction with Tacoma Smelters quiet, and the town was buzzing with rumors of an important discovery. There was much curiosity on the dock as the two men loaded their boat with a tent, blankets, food, and other supplies provided by their grubstaker, Mr. DeGroff, owner of the general store in Sitka. They had a twenty-foot double ended boat with a sail rigged for rowing. They had to journey about fifty miles from the northern part of Baranof, where Sitka was located, to Flag Bay on Chichagof, where they would disembark and hike the few miles to the site. Though they had set out alone early in the morning, about two-thirds of the way they noticed a boat gaining on them. They soon recognized it as the gasoline boat they had seen in Sitka several times, the first motor-powered boat in Southeast Alaska, which was owned by two white men. After the two men with Mr. Beck had landed and were headed up the trail, carrying the usual hunting rifles, they noticed the occupants of the other, faster boat, which had arrived about the same time they had, walking along the nearby ridge in the same direction. By then the outsiders had a good idea where the discovery would be, and the native men were afraid they would jump the claim.

"What happens if they get there before us?" Mr. Beck asked.

"We'll take care of that," said one with a sly look as he patted his gun. Mr. Beck knew for sure then that he wanted no part of a gold mine. They arrived at the site of the gold in the stream without interference and found a vein seven feet wide, with the paystreak down the center. The walls of the fissure had high percentage rock.

Mr. Beck surveyed the area and staked it for them. But when he re-

Interm Superintendent

turned to Sitka, he and the two men approached William Kelly, superintendent of the Sitka Training school, who filed the claim for them under the terms offered. Years later, after the original owners sold their shares for what was considered a large sum of money in those days, Mr. Beck, who had since been ordained a minister and had his own church, was asked why, if he was not interested in the money personally, had he not accepted his share in the name of the church. It would have accomplished so much where money was so badly needed. But he remained convinced that the church was better off not hassling over gold. The Good Lord would provide, he said.

By selling the gold, the owners were able to work the mine with no added capital. Over $21 million worth of gold was taken out within a few years. The claim was never litigated.

Much less exhilarating short items in later papers comment on the lives of the Becks. One item said they had entertained Dr. and Mrs. Wilbur and Miss Gibson at dinner. The March 15, 1902 issue announced that Mrs. Beck and her small daughter left on the Cottage City for a visit to her old home in Kansas, and the June 21 issue reported that Mr. Beck would visit his home in Eldred, New York. "Mr. Beck has been in Sitka for the past eight years and this being his first trip to the states, we are somewhat uneasy to let him make the trip without a trail guide."

The 1901-1902 US Bureau of Education reported an enrollment of 131 at Sitka Training School with W.A. Kelly still as superintendent, and three new teachers: Miss Lizzie Kadashan, Miss Mary Langabear, and J.P.Latourette. Reverend W. S. Bannerman was minister. But Dr. Wilbur had left, and Esther Gibson was serving as the medical missionary at the hospital until his replacement arrived.

The report also stated that there were children in attendance from twelve different tribes, one of several reasons for having the children speak English at the school. Classes were progressing well and industrial work was going satisfactorily. "A band of boys under an efficient industrial teacher is preparing additional land for cultivation for the coming year, clearing it of stumps and other obstructions, and during the coming spring it will be cultivated and planted to grains and vegetables adaptable to Alaskan climate." One of the public schools in Sitka reported that in January and February the girls of the two higher classes went twice a week to a cooking

Interm Superintendent

class taught by Miss Olga Hilton at the Sitka Industrial School.

On December 27, 1902, the Alaskan announced that George Beck and family returned home on the Bonita that day after an extended visit to their old homes in the East. The article failed to mention, however, that they were accompanied on their return by their second child, a boy and the future mayor of Ketchikan, George H. Beck, who was born August 5, while Mrs Beck was in Joplin, Missouri. Previous papers had similarly failed to announce Kosseyia's birth in March of 1898.

By 1904, nine years after his arrival at the Sitka Training school, the Alaskan reported that Mr. Beck had been appointed temporary superintendent of the school upon the departure of W. A. Kelly, who had been serving as superintendent since 1898. By this time the twenty-six-year-old school was a recognized cultural force in Southeastern Alaska. In October of 1904 acting Superintendent George Beck received a letter seeking to hire a student educated there.

> *Dear Brother,*
> *Have you any native girl at Sitka whom you can recommend for school teacher in a small school at Tee Harbor? Need one right away. Salary $60 a month, house rent free. Kindly let me know at once.   Sincerely yours, T.F. Jones*

A month later, Mr. Beck received another letter from Mr. Jones, pastor of the native church at Juneau. The letter said, in asking admission for a small Indian boy: "You will from this on, receive more or less sons and daughters of your former pupils, thus commencing with the second generation. These ought to advance farther than their fellows. And may they."

In the fall of 1904 quite a correspondence took place between Mr. Beck and Dr. George McAfee, school superintendent for the Home Missions Board, regarding teachers' salaries. One letter from the Home office, dated September 21, gives an interesting insight into costs and salaries.

> *At the meeting of the Woman's Board yesterday, the question of the reorganization of the Sitka School in the matter of putting it on the same basis as the other boarding schools so far as the teachers' mess is concerned was considered, and the following recommenda-*

Interm Superintendent

tions were adopted:

First. That the salary of the physician should be made $500 per year and board.

Second. That the salary of the teachers should be made $400 per year and board.

Inasmuch as the board is estimated in our other boarding schools as worth $150 per year, and because of the high price of food in Sitka, it will probably cost the Woman's Board this amount, which means an increase of $50 a year in the salary of the teachers.

We are also authorized to commission Mrs. Saxman as Science Cooking teacher, and by this mail an application will be forwarded, which you will kindly see that she has properly filled out.

The matter of a laundress was considered, but it was decided to defer that until after Dr. McAfee's return, which will probably be in about a month.

The matter of the purchase of the cow and other property belonging to the teachers' mess was deferred also until Dr. McAfee's return, with the thought that in view of the increase of salary it was possible the teachers might be willing to donate this to the Woman's Board. But that will be settled later.

No superintendent has yet been secured for Sitka, but we are hoping one may be found before too long. (Signed) Eleat Boole

A letter from Dr. McAfee dated November 7 thanked the teachers for the gift of the cow to the missions. The teachers evidently donated funds from their recent raise.

Sheldon Jackson wrote two letters to Mr. Beck in October. The first, dated October 24, dealt with building a teachers' residence.

Dear Mr. Beck,

The Secretary of the Interior has authorized the erection of a teacher's residence for the use of the teacher of the native school at Sitka, at an expense not to exceed $1500. While the building will belong to the native school district, yet as long as the teacher of the native school is an unmarried lady and there are one or two other ladies connected with the school that would like accommodations, there will be no objection to the occupation of the building by the

Interm Superintendent

three young women, Miss Rich having the choice of rooms as the building is attached to her school.

If you can find it convenient to erect the building with your carpenter boys and thus give them exercise in real work, the government will make the contract with you for the same. Kindly at your early convenience send me a rough plan of a front elevation, together with plans for ground floor and second story. I would make it neat but plain. Do not want any extra finishings, such as moldings around the window and door frames, or brackets on the outside under the eaves. Have everything plain but substantial and comfortable.

In order that you may be getting material together, when I receive your letter, if it is satisfactory with the Commissioner, I will telegraph you to go ahead.

I wrote both Governor Brady and Mr. Kelly to select a good site for the same, but have heard from neither of them on the subject; they will however both be in Sitka about the holidays and then you can select a good site. In the mean time you can be looking around yourself for a good location.

With kind regards to you wife and the teachers, I remain.
Signed Sheldon Jackson,
General Agent for Education in Alaska

Another letter from Sheldon Jackson dated October 26 told Mr. Beck that Governor Brady and Mr. Kelly had selected a site and were sending plans of buildings to be erected at Presbyterian missions in Killisnoo, Klukwan, and Haines.

"I also send you specifications furnished by the architect. I suspect however that while they might do for this section of the country that they are not the best specifications for Alaska. Kindly look them over and if you do not think they are the best we could have, please write out a new set of specifications and send them to me, and I will have a number of copies made of them and then have advertisements in the Southern Alaska papers for building bids." He ended by reminding Mr. Beck to employ some other qualified native students to help build the residence.

A letter from Dr. McAfee dated December 10 concerned the best way to get fuel for the stoves, coal or wood, which he left to Mr. Beck's discre-

Interm Superintendent

tion. A December 16 letter had several different concerns, not the least of which was the welfare of the cows and chickens.

> *I wrote you yesterday in regard to another matter. I now have your letter of 3rd inst., in which you speak of various repairs and improvements now going forward and need for others. I am sure you will use all the economy possible in making these repairs and improvements, as indicated in my last letter and confirmed by your statement in you letter of 3rd inst.*
>
> *I am glad you consolidated the cow barns. That was one thing that was greatly needed. I hope the cattle are well cared for and have a comfortable place, as they need special care in the winter months.*
>
> *I believe it was understood that when you pulled down the chicken house it was to be removed to some other location, so that you could use the present land for a garden next spring. I hope you will be able, with the lumber taken out of the old building and other old lumber on hand, to provide a comfortable house for the chickens. It seems to me that this is a business that might be almost indefinitely enlarged at the school. There is no reason why you should not only raise all the chickens you need for the table and eggs for the use of the school, but also have eggs for sale. I think the land you are clearing will raise wheat and oats, which could be utilized for chicken feed.*
>
> *I am glad also that you have had the good sense to turn away those boys who misbehaved. You should be careful to make them understand that they are turned away because of misbehavior, and that it is a disgrace to them to be thus dismissed from the school. So with the girls also.*

Finally on March 15, 1905, Dr. George F. McAfee wrote to Mr. Beck: "I believe we have found just the right man for superintendent. He is W.G. Beattie of Oregon City." Mr. Beattie was no stranger to Alaska, McAfee explained. He had had charge of the public school in Wrangell and had learned to love Alaska and believe implicitly in her future. "The more we hear of Mr. Beattie, the better pleased we are. He has the right spirit, a strong physique, and will be able to endure the work that a superintendent is required to do in Sitka." Both these qualities were certainly a must for working in Alaska at that time.

SHELDON JACKSON SCHOOL

The years between 1908 and 1912 saw dramatic changes at the Sitka Training school that included Mr. Beck's improvement of the flume and water system, leading eventually to lighting for the school, the closing of the school in 1911 to facilitate building an entire new plant, and the ordination of Mr. Beck to the ministry and his assignment to Kake as pastor of the mission there.

In 1908 the first volume of the Thlinget was published, replacing the defunct North Star, with George J. Beck editor. The first and second pages list duties of all teachers. Superintendent W.G. Beattie was supervisor of the institution and principal of the school. Assistant Superintendent George J. Beck was also in charge of the Industrial Department, a work of great importance to him because of its significance in the ultimate development of independence for the people. His cherished dream was to see the development of profitable industry in Southeast Alaska. Beck's duties included planning and drafting new work and machinery, overseeing construction work, and teaching a class in bench carpentry. He also did duty as instructor of engineering while waiting for a teacher and as such oversaw the laundry boiler and machinery, the 40-horse hoisting engine, and the saw mill and water system with its two wheels, pumps, and tanks. As commandant of the Training School, he held semi-weekly practice of the drill company, one of the popular features of the school.

The July 1908 Thlinget discussed a meeting of the Presbytery with the Reverend David Waggoner presiding, in which the Reverend David Holford, B.D., was elected moderator and W.G.Beattie, commissioner to the General Assembly, with George J. Beck as alternate. The August issue commented on a visit by US bank examiner and Inspector of national banks in Alaska W.A. Kelly, a former longtime superintendent of the Training School, who was in Sitka to inspect the local banks.

That year's government report listed Mrs. M. Schuknecht as the new girls' matron and several new teachers: H.B. Parks and D. C. McTavish, industrial teachers; Miss Edith Toon and Miss B. M. Chace, teachers; Miss B.M. Kale, teacher of sewing; Misses A. M. Sheets and Olive Kale, kitchen matrons; Miss M. Taner laundry teacher; George McKay bandleader. The October 1908 issue reported that the new sawmill was "in place and in

Sheldon Jackson School

running order" and that instructor Mr. H. B. Parks taught practical saw milling and kept up the fuel supply.

An EXTRA edition in November announced that William Taft had been elected president (it took weeks for the news to reach Sitka). Native troops and the Marines kept order in the streets to prevent riots during the celebration.

According to the November 1908 Thlinget, "The New Covenant Legion has been organized for a number of years..... Mr. Beck was instrumental in organizing the Legion and has been untiring in his efforts to help the people give up the old life and enter the Christian life." Matilda Paul worked with him on this project. In 1913 after Reverend Beck had left Sheldon Jackson, the Alaska Native Brotherhood was organized. William Paul, an early member and president of the ANB, stated in a 1965 letter to George Herbert Beck, that the ANB grew out of the Covenant Legion, which was begun by his mother Matilda Paul and Reverend George Beck.

The March issue announced that the flume at the carpenter shop was still empty as the ice had not yet melted. The progress of the new flume, which would carry the water to power the water wheel and generate electricity, was discussed in the October and November editions of the Thlinget. The October paper reported, "Messrs. Beck, McTavish, and Parks, with the larger boys, are rebuilding the dam (on the Indian River) that was washed out by rains. The dam is more than half-finished." The November paper continued, "For two months, three teachers and the older boys have been building a concrete dam and enlarging the water ditch to harness the power of the Indian River to drive a dynamo to furnish all the buildings with electric lights." A (Pelton) turbine water wheel had been ordered and was expected to arrive by the time the ditch was completed and accessories of the light plant were in place. These issues of the paper also informed their readers that the drill team was practicing regularly and that some of the older girls had entertained friends at a Halloween party at the home of Mr. and Mrs. Beck.

A much more momentous announcement from the Thlinget followed: "The Board has asked for fifty thousand dollars with which to make our school an up-to-date and completely equipped institution for the industrial education of our native Alaskans. At present more that half that amount is assured. . . .The money for this work comes wholly from gifts by individu-

Sheldon Jackson School

als, societies, Sunday schools or churches. Enough has been received that the beginning of the new places are assured." Mr. Beck and Mr. Parks were making a topographical survey of the mission land surrounding the buildings for the Board in New York so that they might be able to give proper directions on the location of the new buildings.

The December 1909 Thlinget commented on the progress of the water-power project. Carpenters under the supervision of carpentry teacher Mr. McTavish were at work removing the engine house to make room for the new power house that would shelter the water wheel and electric light plant. The January 1910 issue featured a story, "Sitka Builders," accompanied by pictures describing the progress of the power project. The first step had been to construct the dam, which took 45 tons of concrete. Next came digging a 3,000-foot ditch through solid rock, frozen dirt, and swamp. By that time the 370-foot long, 26-inch wood stave penstock, made up in the wood shop, had been put in place, leading downhill from the ditch to the Pelton wheel. All the boys old enough to handle a pick or shovel—about twenty-four of them—were working all the time that could be given to it, steadily in rain, snow, and sunshine. On weekdays, however, they worked only after their formal education in the morning.

Although the new water power system was not yet working by March

Penstock Stave Pipe. Ketchikan Museum 71.7.14.29A.

Sheldon Jackson School

Crew Digging Ditch.

Sheldon Jackson School

1910, according to the Thlinget, the carpenters were making headway on the power house, which was 45 feet by 50 feet, large enough to contain the turbine wheel and the dynamo (electric generator) driven by the turbine.

Christmas activities were also reported. On Christmas Eve residents of the cottages caroled the townspeople. Santa appeared on a sleigh at a party for the training school children. A Christmas dinner for the faculty and staff was held at Pittsburgh Cottage, home of Mr. and Mrs. Beattie, featuring hand-decorated menus tied with red ribbon and a sprig of evergreen and a chicken entree—a rare treat. Presents, one for each person in attendance, were hung on a tree in the hall. Guests included were Mr. and Mrs. Gamble and baby Mary; Mr. and Mrs. George Beck with Kosseyia and George Herbert; Mr. and Mrs. Parks, Jean, and baby Parks.

The same paper commented that Mr. Beck had installed a four-horse Fox engine in his boat that for years had been driven by "a daddy might and windjammer motor" [oars and sail]. First had come the bill of lading and note: "Dear Sir, On order of B.K.Wilbur of Philadelphia, Pennsylvania, we have sent you one of our engines as per bill of lading enclosed. We trust that same arrives promptly and in good condition." Then came the notice on the engine, "The last steamer brought a beautiful little four-horse power gas engine all fitted for salt water and ready to be installed. This is the way some men do missionary work, without fuss or feathers, but in a way that tells." At the same time the boys in his carpentry class were building a desk for the primary school room and a large sink for the kitchen.

The February 1910 Thlinget referred to the great activity in the training school boat shop. The entire school fleet was being overhauled and painted. Mr. Beck's boat, with its new house, engine, and name, was to make a fitting flagship for the flotilla. The Fox was launched March 16, 1910, a bright sunny day, and on its trial trip ran through a school of porpoise up to four feet long, delighting those aboard for several minutes. Mrs. Park and McTavish helped Mr. Beck take the boat from the shop to the beach, where it would float when the tide came in—about 12:50 in the afternoon. The whole school was on hand to hear first chug and cheer. Three teachers who were on board lifted the anchor. All hurrahed as the Fox circled the bay and came to the wharf. Kosseyia and George Herbert went on board and many of the students and teachers were given a ride.

A later issue described two trips made in the Fox by Mr. and Mrs Beck,

Sheldon Jackson School

Kosseyia, and several of the teachers to the sealers camp in Biorka. As they entered Symmonds Bay they came upon a large clearing made by the Russians years before when they had had a pilot station there. Towering above the spruce were two masts erected by the Government for an experimental wireless station. For the first trip the weather was glorious, but for the second they had to battle a storm which arose while they were on their way and both boat and passengers proved their seaworthiness.

The April issue had a front page story on W.A. Kelly, superintendent of the training school from 1898 to 1904, who subsequently held the position of superintendent of the US public schools in SE Alaska before becoming a bank examiner. This story discussed the development of the Chichagof Gold Mining Company of which Mr. Kelly had been secretary and treasurer, but with which he had severed connections in the fall of 1908.

The August of 1910 Thlinget ran a startling banner headline on its first page: THE SITKA TRAINING SCHOOL HAS CLOSED ITS DOORS FOREVER! The story continued: The SHELDON JACKSON SCHOOL will stand ready to carry on the work so nobly done in the old buildings. That name would be made official the following year. By 1910 the original buildings had become so inadequate that the Board of Home Missions decided to close the Sitka Training School temporarily in order to build a larger, more efficient plant. The article outlined some of the plans for new buildings and recounted that the Boys' Home, the first building to be erected, was built by Dr. Jackson in 1881 out of lumber he got from a wrecked fish cannery at old Sitka. "The Girls' Home was built of logs and old and new lumber in 1884. The laundry was made of a lot of old sheds about twenty years ago and equipped with second-hand machinery that has been patched until now only the patches remain." After the pupils left for their homes in August of that year, a contractor and force of men began the work of constructing four dormitories, a heating plant, a laundry, an up-to-date schoolroom and a gymnasium.

The same paper featured a story and picture of the drill team, which had been under the command of George Beck for fifteen years. The school was on a military system, wherein the sergeants looked after the conduct of the boys in the absence of teachers and served in many ways to preserve order.

One column included a number of interesting facts about the school at

Sheldon Jackson School

Drill team with Mr. Beck (left) and Dr. Wilbur.   Ketchikan Museums 71.7.14.3

that time. "We have ample water power to furnish all power and light for the entire institution. We have an abundance of pure drinking water, being connected with both our own and the city water systems. . . . .We have a brass band of twenty members and a glee club of fifteen members. We have a girls' choral club of sixteen members. . . The girls in the sewing room are turning out some of the finest work that has ever gone through that department. In addition to their regular work mending they are making dresses and other things that are as near perfection as can be made." The girls had just finished making uniforms for the baseball players and for George Herbert.

In the September issue there was word from Mr. Beck that he and the family had had a fine trip south and were en route to Joplin, Missouri, for a visit with Mrs. Beck's parents, and in October he wrote that they had gone to New York to see his relatives. During this time, according to the January 1911 Thlinget, "Assistant Superintendent George J. Beck was vis-

Sheldon Jackson School

iting the Carlisle Indian School in Pennsylvania to observe the school's work methods, courses of study, and equipment with a view to the further enlargement of his school in Sitka." Mr. Beck had spent a good deal of his time in the United States making speaking appearances on behalf of the Alaska missions. By June of the same year it was announced that the new buildings were completed. Superintendent Beattie had left, and George Beck, who was attending the General Assembly in Atlantic City, New Jersey, as lay commissioner, would return to the training school for the next year as acting superintendent for a second time.

By the time of the 1910-1911 report to the US Bureau of Education, Sheldon Jackson had been replaced by Mr. Lopp as General Agent of Education. Mrs. Patton's report for that year gives a good sense of the teaching situation in Sitka then. "There are about 150 children of school age in the village. About two-thirds of them are enrolled in

Baseball team; George H.

Sheldon Jackson School

any one month, while the average attendance is much less. We have missed our Indian policeman during the past year. I hope that we may soon have a compulsory school law.Such a law would be a benefit not only to the child, but to the parent on whom it would place a responsibility.'

She continued further along, "During the year we have had a most successful cooking class, much interest being shown even by the older women. The dressing room to the bathroom was also used as a laundry three days a week. Many of the women bring their tubs and washboards to make use of the hot water. I consider this our best settlement wedge, for thus the mothers become coworkers with us. [Even then teachers saw the value of involving mothers in their pupils' education.] I procured the services of an experienced laundress to give us instruction in starching and ironing the different kinds of garments. The class was so popular some of the white ladies suggested that they might come too."

"The baths have grown in popularity ever since their opening last year. The young men of my evening class were the first to try bathing frequently, but a few times last year we had a whole household to come. Conservative elderly women were slow to adopt the innovation, but now we have a number who come regularly. It is now quite the fashion, when guests arrive from another town, to bring them to the schoolhouse for a bath."

Later in the report, Miss Patton wrote, "Our village is on a slope rising from the sea. Its superior sanitary condition is largely due to a seawall built of rocks the whole length of the village, the construction of which is a credit to Mr. Brady and my father, who assisted the natives in building it. This, with a four-foot walk built by the natives themselves, adds much to our town. Last year they widened out a narrow back street, even cutting through a house to do it."

Further along she continued, "Our people are quite well-to-do. 'When the tide is out, the table is set.,' for then there are clams, seaweed, and fish eggs to be had for the gathering. The natives provide for future needs by drying fish during the summer and fall. This, with venison, is the principal native article of diet during the winter. In the early spring is the harvest of herring roe, which they collect on boughs and dry. They supply this delicacy to other villages, receiving as much as $1 a sack for it. During the summer berries and fish are in abundance.

"Men women and children work in the canneries, the boats from two

Sheldon Jackson School

places coming for them about the first of June. Some of the men work in the mines at Chichagof and Douglas. During the last year many have worked for the contractor of the new mission buildings, some receiving from 35 to 40 cents an hour. . .Some go trapping in January. Among the villagers, also, are carvers, silversmiths, and moccasin and basket makers, who prepare for the tourist trade in the summer. These are the various ways by which the natives earn the means to buy store clothes, canned goods, and graphophones, of which there are a number in the village. At present the ambition seems to be to own a gasoline launch. There are about a dozen built and owned by natives.

"The utmost cordiality exists between the people and the school. The schoolhouse has come to be quite a settlement house. The village orchestra comes here to use my piano in their practices, and I hope to have a reading room by next year."

Miss Patton was a prime example of the resourceful, generous type of teacher that Mr. Lopp had said in the introduction to his report was called for in Alaska, " teachers well equipped and actuated in the highest degree by altruistic motives. . . The Board of Education strives to obtain for its Alaska school service teachers of good educational qualifications, success in teaching, upright character, philanthropic motives, strong common sense, good health, and a capacity to do effective work under adverse conditions."

There was a concern for the whole person in education that sounds like our present day emphasis. "The work of the Bureau of Education in Alaska, conducted for the benefit of adults as well as children, is practical in character, emphasis being placed on the development of domestic industry, household arts, personal hygiene, village sanitation, morality, and the elementary English subjects." In addition to routine schoolroom work, teachers were expected to perform other duties assigned by the superintendent for the benefit of the natives.

At the end of his report, Mr. Lopp made recommendations that the teachers and staff at the Industrial School would gladly have endorsed. The first was that the natives needed protection from bad influence exerted on them by unprincipled white men. Second, further funds were needed for checking disease among natives. Third, Natives should have the right to own land. Fourth, a compulsory school attendance law should be enacted. Fifth, a seagoing vessel should be supplied to deliver teachers and supplies to the far reaches of Alaska.

On June 7, 1911, the new buildings were completed and the name of the institution was changed to Sheldon Jackson School. At this time Mr. Beattie tendered his resignation in order, he said, "to give opportunity for a new superintendent to administer affairs under new conditions." As early as February 1911 Mr. Beck had tendered his resignation from Sheldon Jackson to Dr. Boyd, the Board of Home Missions superintendent of schools, to take effect no later than April 1911. But he was persuaded to return as interim superintendent upon Mr. Beattie's departure and again took charge of the school until the arrival of the new superintendent, Mr. E. L. Bridgham.

Then the June 1911 Thlinget announced, " Word has just been received that Mr. George J. Beck and his family would start for Sitka immediately after the meetings of the General Assembly at Atlantic City, New Jersey, to which he was Lay Commissioner. Mr. Beck, who has been assistant superintendent of our school for several years, has been in the states for the past nine months speaking in the interest of Alaskan missions. He will now return to the Sheldon Jackson School and have charge here until a superintendent is appointed."

On August 16 the Thlinget had an announcement dear to the heart of Mr. Beck; for the first time in history Sheldon Jackson was lighted by electricity. The flume and waterwheel were doing their work! God had said "Light!' and there was light. But God had worked through his emissary, Mr. George J. Beck. Coming up with the idea of the waterwheel was divinely inspired. He had had no previous experience with such things, although he had learned the tools of his trade. The physical work and knowledge of how to improvise probably came from Mr. Beck's youthful indentureship, where the worker had to think on his feet and use all the skills he possessed. There were no how-to books in those days.

In the fall of 1911 letters arrived from Kosseyia, who had been left with relatives to go to school in the East when the Becks visited earlier that year. One from Phoenicia, New York, dated September 24 thanked her mother for her letter and mentioned that she would love to hear from her dad, although she understood how busy he was. She told of staying overnight with her grandmother, who she thought was lonesome, and of outings that her aunts and uncles were taking. She herself sounded a little lonely, as she said she wished she could be going with them on some of the

Sheldon Jackson School

trips. She also wished she could be going on the picnics the family at home was having. A letter dated September 25 to her "dear, dear brother" thanked him for his letter and asked about school: "Who is your teacher? How do you like her? I have a very funny teacher. I like my school pretty well—better than at first." and further on, "I hope you will tell me all about the new buildings. I am so anxious to see them." She then told about seeing a porcupine and a woodchuck. She got to drive part way up and down from the camp and thought it was fun to drive a horse.

The January 1912 Thlinget ran a large banner headline in inch-deep print: THERE ARE BETWEEN 25 AND 30,000 NATIVE PEOPLE IN ALASKA TERRITORY. ALL ARE SELF SUPPORTING. Then in half-inch type: A MAJORITY OF THE YOUNGER GENERATION CAN READ AND WRITE. THOUSANDS OF THEM ARE LIVING IN CLEAN UP-TO-DATE HOMES MANY OPERATE SMALL STORES. Then in smaller headline type: "They run gas boats for hire and are earning a livelihood in many of the standard trades. They do pay taxes at the same rate the white men do but are not allowed to hold land, locate mining claims, or enjoy the rights and privileges of American Citizenship." The Thlinget devoted a large part of its space to the question: Should Indians vote? Editor George J. Beck answered. "There is no longer any reason why they should be denied the right to take their place with the people of the earth."

The April 1912 Thlinget reported on the Presbytery meeting at Wrangell and announced that George J. Beck, who had recently been ordained a minister, would take over the ministry at Kake, recently vacated by the Friends (Quakers). Finally the June issue announced that G. J. Beck would be leaving the Sitka Industrial School. "George J. Beck, after eighteen years in the work of the Sitka school, has been commissioned pastor of the church at Kake Village, Alaska, and expects to start with his family about the first of July for the new station. Mrs. Beck entered the work of the Sitka Training School January, 1883, nearly twenty years ago."

An agreement addressed to the Reverend George J. Beck and dated May 12, 1912 reads: The Presbyterian Church and congregation of Kake in connection with and on the recommendation of the Presbytery of Alaska having made application for aid in your support as their Minister, the Board hereby commissions you a Missionary to the above-named field, to which you have been appointed by the Presbytery for the term of seven months from September 1, 1912, and agrees to pay you seven hundred dollars ($700) from its treasury for services rendered in accordance with the subjoined rules.

"It is further agreed that the minister shall give his full time to the entire field to which he has been appointed by the Presbytery, and this agreement shall become void by a failure to preach regularly at any preaching places named in it, or by exchanging any such places for others not herein mentioned, or by the disapproval by Presbytery of the minister or his work signified by action on its part.." Signed by the President D. Stuart Dodge.

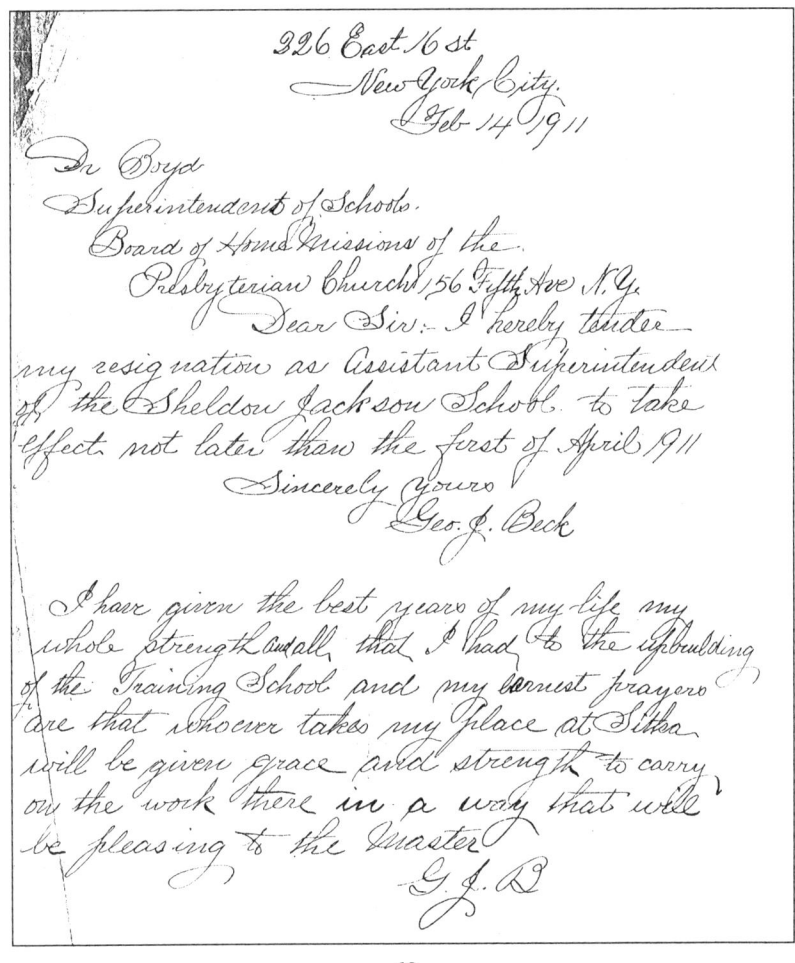

KAKE AND HOONAH

As it turned out, although he did serve as interim superintendent for six months after Sheldon Jackson reopened and finished the year as industrial teacher, George J. Beck left the school as it was embarking on a renewed life in new buildings and with a new administration. He had always wanted to do missionary work, and at last his goal was achieved. In 1912 he was ordained a Presbyterian minister and assigned to a mission at Kake that had just been vacated by the Quakers.

After a visit to the Weaver and Beck families in Joplin and New York, the Becks moved to Kake and the ministry started right away. Their daughter Kosseyia, who was 14 years old at the time, was left with an aunt in New York to go to school in the East, but nine-year-old George accompanied them to Kake.

After a dramatic introduction to Kake, Mr. and Mrs. Beck were to spend four-and-a-half years there before being assigned briefly to Hoonah and then taking a leave to serve as a civilian chaplain in the military during World War I. In Kake they operated the Lois, a 55-foot gasoline launch with an auxiliary sail. This mobile home made it possible to get around to the native settlements whenever they were needed. Other early boats the

The Lois.

Kake and Hoonah

Beck Family at Prayer Service Camp.

Missions operated in Southeast included the Princeton, the A.L. Lindsley, the Good Tidings, and much later, the Princeton-hall.

The Becks had not been in Kake long when they were awakened one morning to find the natives burning the totem poles. Of course they were astounded at the devastation before them. When Mr. Beck asked what had

Prayer Service at Fishing Camp..

brought it about, all involved explained that they had agreed among themselves that destroying the totem poles was the best way to begin a new Christian life. Excerpts from a letter which was written by George J. Beck over thirty years later and printed in the 1963 edition of Edward Keithahn's *Monuments in Cedar*, attempted to answer the author's questions about the event. According to Keithahn, the letter "clarifies the matter of the destruction of the totem poles and throws much light on the position, the difficulties, and the problems of the pioneer missionaries on the Northwest Coast:"

> *After eighteen years on the faculty of the Sitka Training school, afterwards the Sheldon Jackson school, I was ordained by the Presbytery of Alaska and sent to Kake in the summer of 1912. Kake was about sixty-five miles from the nearest peace officer or doctor. Mrs. Beck and I were met with black looks and all anyone would say was, "We don't know you; we will wait and see what you are going to do." All the people seemed greatly discouraged; their sidewalks and large tribal houses were falling to pieces; fighting and heavy drinking was the order of the day. The whites of the whole country round were afraid of them. The Kake natives were unjustly blamed for the disappearance of any white man who happened to be shipwrecked or lost in that part of the country. The people were tired of their way of life and wanted to change.*
>
> *There were many totem poles in Kake then; large crude affairs, and a number of so-called mortuary poles, but as far as I could see there was nothing in them but just a handful of well-burnt ashes so there would be no question of burning them for sanitary reasons. The custom of cremation had been given up many years before, as can be proved by the great number of graves on the two islands just in front the village when we arrived there in 1912.*
>
> *Kake was about equally divided between the Salvation Army under the leadership of Charles Newton and his wife (as fine a young native couple as I ever met) and the Friends mission. The Friends church and mission buildings had just been sold to the Board of Home Missions of the Presbyterian Church without consulting the members of the church and they felt that had been sold out, so my position in the village was anything but secure.*

Kake and Hoonah

Charlie Gunnuk was the main leader of the Friends church and he was a very fine old gentleman. I am sure that neither he or the Friends church were the leaders in the burning of the poles. After a few months of hard work the leaders of both organizations came to me with this story and request. They said both the Salvation Army and the church have broken down, our people have become "backsliders." We are afraid, something must be done, we cannot do it alone. Will you help us and tell us what to do? Nothing was said about totem poles; they were a thing of the past; they did not enter into the picture either in the minds of Charles Newton, Charlie Gunnuk or my own. Many of the poles were out of sight anyway, covered with brush and trees. We went to work. The people had a very able brass band but like everything else they had given up practice, and feasts for the dead and drunken dances had taken over everything.

I called a meeting of the whole town, told them the only practical way out was the spiritual life through Christ Jesus and then put on a regular political campaign. We turned out the band, nominated a large number of candidates and elected twelve men for a council and then the twelve men appointed a town marshal and city magistrate, built a jail, and set the town on its feet. We asked the Governor of Alaska if we could be given any legal standing and he said, "You have no legal standing and can't be given any but there is such a thing as government with the consent of the governed and if the people want it that way, KEEP UP THE GOOD WORK and I will back you up if things get out of hand."

All this time the poles were sleeping quietly in the brush. One morning I was awakened with the feeling that something unusual was taking place. Rushing out, I found the place covered with smoke and nearly all the poles blown up and burned. One pole was still standing in the churchyard. I asked what they were going to do with it. They said it is yours; do what you like with it; when I refused to touch it, they burned it with the rest. The whole village took part in the work but no one would admit giving the orders. They said they wanted to clean up and get rid of the old life that was not good. I have not kept a record of these doings but as the poles were all there in 1912 and gone in 1914, they must have burned in 1913.

Kake and Hoonah

And now comes the strange part of the story, but like everything else connected with the totem pole, I have nothing to prove it but I believe it to be true. There was living in Kake at that time an old Indian Doctor. The people had lost faith in him but he still held some power over them and sometime after the burning of the poles I was told he could see the old life was changing; one after another the old customs were going out and unless he did something drastic he would go out with the rest of the old ways. So he told the people that his spirit had discovered an evil spirit lurking in the ashes of the departed in the old poles and unless they destroyed all the totems the whole village would be wiped out. The people, having lost interest in the poles and wanting to get rid of them anyway, obeyed the doctor.

I have been so busy trying to lead this fine people out of the darkness they were in that I have spent very little time taking pictures. I have nothing on the Kake poles or any others; in fact, a missionary in those days was not supposed to have money enough to buy equipment, and the powers that be saw to it that he did not have salary enough to lead him into temptation.

It is hard to imagine what kind of life the young family had in this small village. George Herbert attended the school there, where he quickly made friends with the other children, all of whom were native. There was a general store where they could buy groceries and other supplies and a cannery out the road some distance from the town where most of the men probably worked.

Though Kosseyia was in the East, she was never far from the minds of her family, nor they from hers. In a letter dated July 12, 1912, when the Becks had been in Kake for almost a year, she remarked that George H. would soon be ten years old and wished him a happy birthday. She had just heard from a letter Mrs. Beck had written Reverend Beck's mother that the family had moved to Kake and she wanted George H. to write a long letter telling her all about the village and their life there. She wished she could be with them, and told of going for a row with their Grandma and Grandpa on Stege Lake and being surprised how out of practice she had become in rowing. Grandpa, an artist and sculptor, was having trouble with his arm from working too hard on the grave stones. "How often do you have a

Kake and Hoonah

George Herbert in Kirberger's Store.

boat?" she asked, plaintively it seemed, and ended, "With oceans of love to all."

When Kosseyia first went East, she stayed with her Aunt Lulu and Uncle Herbert Chace, who had a girl Alice, with whom Kosseyia became a lifetime friend, and a younger boy Alfred, who apparently pestered Kosseyia mercilessly. The week before she was to leave for school in Northfield with Alice, she mentioned in a letter to her parents that Aunt Lulu thought Kosseyia, who was then fifteen, should not marry until she was forty-five and then not have children. "I can't get along with children, she says. I think I can with most children. Alfred Chace is an exception. The only trouble is that I don't like to be pinched, punched, poked, and slapped every few minutes."

When he was about twelve, George clerked in the store and pulled a wagon to delivery groceries to the cannery. Mr. Kirberger, the owner, expected good work from George, but was good natured in dealing with him, his greatest threat about an order being, "Get it right, or down comes your meathouse!"

There is a picture of a watch tower George and his father had built from

Kake and Hoonah

which he could survey the waters for miles. His playing at spying turned more serious, however, when he kept a lookout for German warships and submarines after World War I had started in Europe. Another picture shows young George and a friend carrying several ducks that George had bagged with the shotgun his father had given him—probably that night's dinner.

A communication from the Fisherman's Union, which was at that time made up mainly of natives, exhorted Mr. Beck to complete and circulate among the natives an enclosed petition to abolish fish traps that would be sent to Congress in November. The letter ended: "The saving of our food fish from wanton destruction is as important as any question that can possibly come before our people and will require our whole thought and best

George H.'s Watchtower; Lois in Background.

Kake and Hoonah

endeavors." For years he encouraged the natives in their efforts to control the massive overfishing by the canneries, but it was many years before these efforts were successful.

Again it is through letters and newspaper reports that the Becks' activities are revealed while they lived at Kake. Between 1912 and 1918 Kosseyia wrote several letters telling about activities at the Northfield Seminary School in Massachusetts, where she was going to school. There is a letter dated November, 1913, from Kosseyia in East Northfield to her Aunt Sue in New York, which Aunt Sue had sent to Reverend and Mrs. Beck for their enjoyment. Kosseyia expressed the hope that her aunt would be able to come to Northfield for a weekend, but the letter was mainly in reply to one from Aunt Sue asking the sixteen-year-old Kosseyia's size so that she could buy her a corset. "I am a great deal stouter than when I saw you last. I weigh about 150 pounds. My bust measure is 39 inches, waist measure is 27 inches, and hips measure is 40 inches. . .I don't know how to express my appreciation of your kindness. I have looked longingly at corsets which lace in front and wished that I might have one." In the last paragraph Kosseyia expressed her pleasure that Papa and Mama had a new house and that they might be getting a larger boat. Aunt Sue's note to the Becks at the end explained that she had sent Kosseyia two pictures, one of a waist and one of a corset, to get her preference. She also said there was a chance she might be sent to Boston on business and if so would see Kosseyia.

Mrs. Beck Reads Letters.

From a presbytery meeting in Juneau Mr. Beck wrote Hattie a letter dated March 31, 1914, in which he referred to his talks with the governor. "I am having good success so far.

Kake and Hoonah

The Governor goes to Washington D.C. tomorrow, starting this afternoon, and is taking with him several of my postals [pictures] of Kake doings with him. He goes to talk on Indian affairs and I arrived in the nick of time to catch him. He seemed much impressed with my story of the Kake people and has promised to do all in his power to help us. I supplied the pulpit of the First Congregational church (white) of Douglas last Sunday night; their pastor was away preaching."

In a letter dated April 25, 1915, Kosseyia wrote that she was delighted with two letters from her mother, who had been visiting in Ketchikan, and dreaded having her mother go back to Kake, as the less frequent mail service would make the letters fewer. She found the food at the school awful and bemoaned the fact that her two watches had cost more than expected to be repaired. She had to leave the silver one at the jeweler's until she could come up with the $1.50 for its repair. She sympathized with her parents' difficulty in sending George H. to Ketchikan for high school. " It will be dreadfully hard for you to send George Herbert away, but of course it will be the best thing for him."

Young George left Kake in the fall of 1915 at the age of 13 to attend high school in Ketchikan. Arrangements had been made for him to stay with Dr. B. Meyers and his wife a few blocks from the school. A postcard postmarked "5 pm September 3" from Dr. Meyers informed them, "Just a line to say that George arrive about ten minutes ago. Thought you would like to know."

The April 1916 Verstovian, which replaced the Thlinget as school paper, reported a presbytery meeting in Hoonah. The Lois and Good Tidings brought ministers from the outlying areas. Reverend J. S. Clark was elected moderator and took the chair at once. Reverend George J. Beck, outgoing moderator, preached an effective sermon, taking as the text, "I Go Afishing."

Then suddenly a December 1916 issue announced that the reverend George J. Beck had been transferred from Kake to Hoonah. A letter upon his arrival in Hoonah dated November 16, 1916, began:

"Our hook is down and we securely fastened to the bottom of the harbor of Hoonah. We arrived last Monday the 13th after a good trip from Kake. . . .Sunday was spent at Killisnoo and Angoon where we had fine meetings......We were finely received by the people, white

Kake and Hoonah

and native, and made to feel welcome. We conducted the funeral of a little child the first day in. Last night we had one hundred out to prayer meeting. Monday we are to have a very large wedding. We were sorry to leave Kake at this time feeling our work had just reached a point where we could make things show, but as it had to be, we are glad to be here and can see where great good can be done... Now there is one thing I must have as soon as possible and that is a good chain and cement to hold the Lois. I am anchored in five fathoms and now Mr. Good tells me I am a little close to the shore."

A longer letter dated November 24, 1916, informed Dr. Condit, director of the missionaries in Southeast Alaska, of the conditions in Hoonah:

"Your good letter received yesterday. I appreciate your kind words and pray God we may be able to accomplish the work so much needed in this place.

Now to plunge right in I will say it was not my intention to say anything about conditions here but to go at it and do my best to clean things up. I feel now however you should know the situation as it is. In the first place after all this time, the trip to Sitka, the extra trip for the people to come in from the canneries for the election and after the council has been elected, it is now discovered that the whole proceeding was illegal because Mr. Good forgot to post the notices of election and the lawyers in Juneau tell Mr. Richardson that nothing the council could do would hold in the law. Just before we arrived they began all over again by sending to Sitka for permission to hold another election to organize the town. Nothing has been heard from DeArmond as yet. The people are on the ragged edge. They don't know what the mistake was.

Night before last I was called at 11:30 and was soon in a little room about twelve feet square in the midst of a fight with two white men and a native girl (all drunk), three other natives, two Filipino men, and a loaded shotgun. No one was hurt but it looked bad for a time. I have good evidence on the white men and we have them on the run. I was told this morning that the other white men in town feel very badly that the thing happened and have suggested to the bad men that they leave town.

Kake and Hoonah

The people are ready to go ahead and I believe we can accomplish something this winter if we make no mistakes, but we must be on the job every minute. The people will start out [for hunting and fishing] again right after the new year and we will have a very short time to do much.

Mr. Good is at Strawberry Point. We lived on the Lois until he left Saturday afternoon. This is a nice little house on the inside. We like it but the outside and the shed back are in a terrible condition. Mr. Good has the Tornado [boat] and will keep it until called for. He also has the church books and the money, if there is any. He is to take care of Mr. Davis' place this winter while the latter is below and has a cow, chickens, all the potatoes the family can eat besides many other things. A good warm house to live in. He tells me that all through the cold spell last winter the cattle lived outside at Strawberry Point, found their own food, and kept fat. Mr. Good also has use of a team of horses to haul logs to build his house. I would not have mentioned all these things if it had not been that I wanted you to see how important it is that I should be here all the time now.

I should dearly love to go to Skagway with you to organize the church but feel if I am taken away for two weeks at this time I would not be able to do anything this winter and the whole year would be lost. There is something going on every minute. They need a guiding hand so much. Is it possible to organize the church without the presence of the Lois or myself? We have sent Mr. Good away and the people will not understand if I leave now when there is so much to do. Please let me know as soon as possible about the trip, but if possible to do so do not take me away before the first of the year."

A letter dated December 2, 1916, to Dr. Condit mentioned that they had a fine Thanksgiving. " The church was decorated with flags and the band played several pieces and I succeeded in getting Mr. Richardson on the platform to deliver a short address."

A reply to Mr. Beck in January of l917 from Dr. Condit, who was visiting in Ketchikan, informed him that George Herbert had come down with measles. Then several months later Mr. F. Lowle, general agent of the Canadian Pacific Railway Company, wrote him in May concerning the cost to bring Kosseyia to Hoonah. She would have been 19 or 20 years old at

Kake and Hoonah

that time, and still in high school. A lack of much formal education before going east probably required a longer time for her to fulfill graduation requirements.

An announcement from Kosseyia invited her parents to her graduation in June of 1918. Her school yearbook, the June 1918 Northfield Star, had a picture and paragraph about her that stated she would be going to Columbia. However, there was no mention of Columbia in her 1919 letters, although she did refer to her job and her raise to $90 in one of them.

Kosseyia and Parents on the Lois.

Mr. Beck's stay in Hoonah was interrupted for service during World War I when he and Mrs. Beck and George went to New York for Mr. Beck to serve as a YMCA chaplain on a troop ship going to Europe. At 45 years, he was too old to enlist as a naval chaplain, as he would have liked. He was assigned to the USS Mongolia, from which he made nine round trips to France. "He was known at the 'Rustling Chaplain,'" S. Hall Young wrote in an article for the Presbyterian magazine in 1923. "The boys loved him and imposed upon him. He organized moving picture entertainments, dramatic plays, all kinds of stunts for the amusement of the boys and he talked to them the sermon of a consecrated Christian life every day. Conversions were constant. Admirals and Generals became his companions." George Herbert at 14 was too young to enlist, but he did drive a YMCA truck in New York during the war.

A letter dated April 11, 1919, from the Mongolia is entitled "Report from George J. Beck, Transport Secretary."

Sir- We sailed from Hoboken N.J. March 20, 1919, without cargo

Kake and Hoonah

or passengers and for the first time in nine months had a real navy chaplain attached to the ship. I have been acting chaplain to our crew of from five to six hundred men ever since entering upon my duties last year. Since the fighting is finished the Navy has enough chaplains to go round so we now have ours. Our chaplain is of the Catholic Church and seems a very nice fellow. We have very pleasant relations.

While my duties were very much lighter than usual I still found something to do in giving out books to the crew, for we have charge of the A.L.A. books placed on board by that wonderful association. We also gave two picture shows a day, one to the crew and the other to the officers. Of course there were lots of other little things the men wanted and in some way we managed to get it for them.

After a stay of only ten hours in Brest, France, we started back for the States. The return trip was one of our best. Warm spring weather all the way over, very little wind, and no rough sea. I did not hear a word of criticism and every man seemed happy. We tried to see that every man had something to occupy his mind. The weather was so fine we used the picture machine on deck. This allowed two thousand men to assemble at each show, giving us an attendance of about twenty thousand men for the trip. We gave out over two thousand magazines and about twenty cases of A.L.A. books We also distributed enough candy for each man besides gum, apples, oranges, cigarettes and many other things for the five thousand men on board.

Mr. Hodges of the Knights of Columbus and myself work together with the men and in the handling of our supplies find we can do very satisfactory work in this way. We were also assisted by several soldiers and sailors who were of great service.

Very sincerely yours, (signed) George J. Beck

KLUKWAN

The October Verstovian announced that the reverend George J. Beck had returned from war service and would go to the mission in Klukwan, a Tlingit village at the head of Lynn Canal near Haines. Though his stay there lasted less than a year, he accomplished much.

A journal started shortly after his arrival in October, describes his day-to-day routine. Since his home and the church and school buildings were all heated by wood, woodcutting was a daily, demanding job, especially in winter with temperatures frequently below zero. Sometimes he had to walk great distances and, as firewood sources became more scarce, to take a horse and sled or carriage for toting back the wood. Residents thought nothing of walking the twenty-two miles to Haines and back when the occasion warranted. He commented frequently on the beauty of the clear, crisp day, so different from those of the rainy Southeast.

The journal, which begins in late 1919, was probably intended as a record of church work, expenses, and attendance at services. But with each day's entry, the life drama of the village unfolds. The native's original mistrust gradually developed into trust and eventually into friendship and reliance upon Reverend Beck. He was confronted almost daily with death, especially with the influenza epidemic. At first the people he buried were strangers, then many were friends, and finally one was a close friend and supporter. At times he built coffins and dug graves, and at least once he washed the body of a friend and dressed him for burial. Even a little comedy creeps in with comments about his serving as intermediary in arranging a marriage and his problems milking the cow that supplied milk for the school children.

October ll, Saturday: A most beautiful day. Warm sunshine, just above freezing. Direction of wind is north, but very little stirring. About four inches of snow on the ground. No ice in the river. Sold six dollars' worth of shiplap to Walter Shotridge and collected the money. Helped him take it home. Cleaned the church and prepared the stove for Sunday service. Made a number of calls.

October 12, Sunday: Another wonderful day. Held one service in the church at two p.m. with Mrs. Carr at the organ. Bessie Shotridge was the interpreter. Thirty were present, about all the people in town. All the

Klukwan

natives tell me the weather will change and all the snow will go before real winter sets in. I hope they are right.

October 13, Monday: Worked during the morning helping around the house. Assisted Mr. Carr [the teacher] oil his wagon as he was starting for Haines with four passengers. In the afternoon walked a long way above Wells. The afternoon was grand, warm and bright. The wind, what there was of it, was south. Saw a number of mallard ducks, lots of salmon, dead and alive, many bear tracks in the snow, some very large ones, a few rabbit tracks. Two teams arrived with native outfits and brought mail.

October 15, Wednesday: [Note: no entry for Tuesday] Wind south, cloudy but no rain. Helped Mr. Carr rebuild the sidewalk at the store. We took up and rebuilt about one hundred feet of the walk using the old lumber. Three grave stones and one grave fence have arrived already. I suppose there will be lots of them before the people settle down.

October 16, Thursday: Warm and foggy all day. Sun did shine a few minutes this afternoon. Spent the morning cleaning up and getting the small room off the woodshed ready for a carpenter shop. Remodeled small table to be used as a writing desk.

October 17, Friday: Warm sunshine most of the day. Called on one sick old man and helped Mr. Carr get his carrots. He gave me a sack full, which I spread out on the cellar floor to dry out.

October 18, Saturday: Light rain. Started to remodel dining room table. Visited every house in the village and spent the evening at a sociable gotten up by the teachers in honor of Alaska Day.

October 19, Sunday: Warm and pleasant. Held morning service at 10:30 a.m. Forty present. Charles Kladoo rang the bell. Mrs. Carr played and Mr. Carr led in prayer. We spoke on the first chapter of St. John. Mr. Guerin came home with us and gave me five dollars for a broken window and the wood burned while his family stayed at the house. He also took his pew and ammunition. Held our first prayer meeting at 7 p.m. 10 present.

October 20, Monday: Warm, but cloudy. Snow on mountains but none below. Sold 56 feet of Mr. Falconer's lumber at $63 per M to Willard Rouch. Received cash. Did some work on dining room table.

October 21, Tuesday: Went to head of water works to shut off water so Willard Couch could mend pipe in front of his new store. Worked with Mr. Carr. Helped him raise the school toilets. Mr. Chiswell arrived this

Klukwan

evening with another boatload of natives. Jack Means of Hoonah is in town and says the Hoonah Council is doing great.

October 22, Wednesday: Clear and cold all day. Mr. Carr and I walked the trout stream, for about twelve miles and caught a dozen and a half trout. The stream was full but they did not seem hungry. The little fellows would swarm about the hook and steal the bait, but the big ones were too lazy. Mr. Carr shot three fine ducks and gave me one. Mr. Voegle brought mail from Haines: letters from Kosseyia, George H., and Mother Sue.

That weekend natives came from Hoonah for a three-day potlatch. There was a slight earthquake. Fifty people at morning service. Ice was running in the river, still a week away from November. Mr. Beck wrote Dr. Condit saying he would be glad to go to Hoonah if needed. The Carrs would like to go too. Mrs. Carr also taught at the school.

October 27, Monday: Steve Ragen was shot through the heart in Ketchikan. October 29, Steve's body was laid to rest at Haines. Steve Sheldon came to Klukwan today in his car.

October 30, Thursday: Twenty-five men are working on a grave fence in front of Frank White's house. John Benson called this afternoon and made a long visit. Told us the people of Hydaburg, Klawock, and Kake were doing splendid, but did not speak well of the workers here. He wants to marry Mrs. Newman. The next day Mrs. Newman called to ask what I thought about her marriage to John Benson. She wants to marry him but seems a bit doubtful about it. Crossed the river in a canoe with Mr. Carr for six boxes of sand for the concrete to be used in the engine bed. The big boys have started to practice basketball. Frank White gave a $300 dinner, probably to "pay" helpers with the grave fence.

November 2, Sunday: Fifty at morning service. Mrs. Newman called after Sunday school to talk over her matrimonial affairs. Mrs. Bessie Shotridge was her interpreter.

November 3, Monday: Helped Mr. Carr move the light engine down into the school basement.

November 4, Tuesday: Took Prince the government horse out and brought in half a cord of birch wood. We find it almost equal to coal. I set a trap for rabbits. Wrote a letter to Mr. John Benson for Mrs. Newman in regard to marriage license. Officers elected for Sunday school were Sam R. Johnson, superintendent; Mrs. Bessie Shotridge, assistant superinten-

Klukwan

dent; Miss Marian Wilson, secretary; James Johnson, treasurer.

November 6, Thursday: Spent most of the morning on the mountain with Mr. Carr investigating the slide back of the village of Klukwan. There is no possible way of stopping it without spending thousands of dollars. Mrs. Newman and John Benson were married this evening at the manse. Two teams came up this evening with letters from both the children.

Several days followed in which wood was cut, Prince fell in the snow, much fish was caught. The temperature had gone well below freezing. Eighty-five at Sunday service. There were plans to start a town council. On Wednesday, November 12, he talked the matter over with Frank White, who evidently had status in the community. When ideas were presented to the other men all were agreeable to them.

November 13, Thursday: Worked on floor and ceiling of church. Found shoes for Prince that night and planned to nail them on in the morning. There has been much debate about the Council.

November 15, Saturday: Summoned to door at midnight and told of death of young Dan Hotch. A dog team pulled out that night to get a coffin.

November 18, Tuesday: Services for Dan Hotch in the church. He is the third son the Hotches have lost.

November 21, Friday: Frank White and I took the horse and scraper down the snow slide about a mile down the road and cut a passage through. I cut wood in the afternoon to have some ahead when I go to Haines. The Council held a meeting in the Frog House and then called me down about 10 p.m. to tell me they had decided to wait a while before organizing the town. Benson seemed to be the trouble. I talked with them for some time.

November 22, Saturday: I took Prince and the sleigh down to get a load of wood I had cut earlier, but found after crossing the bridge at Wells the snow was about eight inches deep and the sled cut right through to water. So as soon as I got to some alder I stopped and cut a load. After coming home and cleaning up myself and Prince, I headed to the store for a can of oil. Saw Benson down there and told him I heard he was the one who did not want the Council. He became very angry and said he owned the whole town. His grandfather owned the place and it was his. The people are becoming provoked at his attitude in the matter. Joe King called in with Sam Johnson to talk over matters and to assure me he was in favor of the council.

Klukwan

November 24, Monday: Clear and cold. I got up at 2 a.m. and started for Haines with Prince at 4 a.m., cut out two large trees, picked out three slides, and chopped through one glacier. I arrived in Haines about 1 p.m. I got everything ready before the stores closed at 6 p.m. and stayed all night at Reverend Denton's

November 25, Tuesday: Started from Haines at 8:45 a.m. with a bulky but not too heavy load. There was no snow for sixteen miles so I used the wagon, then changed to the sleigh. The day before I left I took the wagon apart and put it on the sled, so I had both the wagon and the sled. When the snow ran out at 16 mile post, I left the sled there and used the wagon.

November 27, Thanksgiving Day: Mrs. Beck and I had dinner with the Carrs, including chicken and ice cream.

November 30, Sunday: Eighty present at services. Ordained church officers: George Willard, Charles Kladoo, William Johnson, Frank White. William Johnson elected treasurer.

December 1, Monday: We held our first session meeting this evening. The newly elected church officers were all present: Elders Charles Kladoo and George Willard; Deacons Billie Johnson and Frank White; treasurer William Johnson and school superintendent Sam R. Johnson and assistant superintendent Mrs. Bessie Shotridge.

December 3, Wednesday: Went up to Wells to see Mr. Donnelly, who has been quite sick for two days.

December 6, Saturday: Went up to Wells this morning to offer my services to the Donnellys, as Mr. Donnelly died last night, but there was nothing to do. They were waiting for Ed Donnelly to come back with the casket. He started for Haines at midnight last night. Mrs. John Willard is quite sick. John has gone for the doctor and Hattie stayed with her all night. I called on all the houses in the village this afternoon. Mr. Willard returned but the doctor would not come, Too busy was his excuse.

December 7, Sunday: Eighty-four present. Beautiful music this morning. Hattie tired after sitting up with Mrs. Willard all night. Mrs. Wilson sick, so I taught all three large classes. Twenty-five at evening service.

December 8, Monday: Hitched up Prince and drove him to Wells for the rough box to cover Mr. Donnelly's coffin. Conducted Donnelly funeral this afternoon. Visited several sick people.

December 11, Thursday: Pete Nelson called for a visit at noon and gave

Klukwan

Mr. and Mrs Beck and Sled.

me a Thlinget lesson. [He lists the 19 members of the Keet clan and their Thlinget names] Milked cow and took milk to school house. Seventy at church and fifty at Sunday school.

On Saturday he fixed a saw for an old lady who lived in the smoke house. The next ten days are concerned with wood cutting and hauling, snow shoveling and building repairs. Two feet of snow on Wednesday. On December 19 the body of Jack Paddie's little girl was brought from Haines.

December 22, Monday: Got up at 4:45 and took old Prince to get a load of birch from below the slide. Built a platform in the church for the Christmas entertainment.

December 23, Tuesday: Mr. Carr and I went with old Prince up the road about half way to Wells to cut the church Christmas tree and other greens. Decorated the church and held rehearsal for the entertainment in the church.

December 24, Wednesday: Got ready for Christmas. Spent the evening at the Frog House. Dinner for the whole town.

Christmas Day: Busy getting ready for dinner. At two p.m. Mr. and Mrs. Carr ate with us. Esten could not leave his father. The entertainment (at the church) was good. Everyone was there. I have been asked to take the census in the area.

December 28, Sunday: Ninety at church

Klukwan

January 6, l920 Tuesday: Started for Haines on foot at one a.m. Very hard going, very slippery and hard south wind and rain from 12 mile down. My packs were very smooth and by the time Haines was reached, I was well used up. Arrived at ll a.m. I turned in the petition for local self-government from the Klukwan people. Went over to Rev. Denton's and rested most of the afternoon and evening. Spent most of Wednesday taking the oath of office as special agent under the Census Bureau.

January 8, Thursday: Started back from Haines at 9:45 a.m. with all the first class mail. The roads were terrible but I had on new creepers and got along nicely. Began my census work on the road up and by the time I reached Mr. Voegle's place it was very dark. He kindly invited me to stay all night which I did and as he was going to Wells for a load of lumber, I planned to ride up with him.

January l0, Saturday: Not very cold. Light snow. Cut wood and made several calls. Did my work for Sunday. Sam Johnson returned from Juneau. Did not get his citizen papers because the Judge was away. The body of George Kelley arrived this evening. Held session meeting this evening.

January 12, Monday: Funeral services for George Kelley at 2 p.m. at the church.

January l3, Tuesday: Jack Lee and Mary Kahtlewa were married in the church at 2 p.m. They were dressed at the manse and marched into the church while the band played. Double ring ceremony. We all attended a supper and social evening given by Mr. and Mrs. Lee at the home of Frank White the same evening.

January l4, Wednesday: As Mr. Carr is at Haines I am caring for the cow. Three below zero this morning. Maggie Ka-den-a-ha delivered my snow shoes this afternoon. They look like new ones. I paid her five dollars to reweave the old ones. Prayer meeting this evening. Very cold and very few out. Charlie Kladoo is too sick to ring the bell.

January l5, Thursday: Fourteen below zero this morning. Milked as Mr. Carr did not return, cut wood. Took axe and snow shoes out, axe to cut wood on the road to Wells and the snow shoes to try them out. They both worked well. The first time I ever tried snow shoes in the woods. I only fell once. It has been standing at 8 below zero all day.

He continues to cut wood every day to get ahead for the census trip.

January l9, Monday: Fifteen below zero. Kitchen stove gave trouble.

Klukwan

The water back froze and cracked one of the returns. I had to take it out of the stove. Was busy all day with cow, wood, and water. This evening we held council meeting at Frank White's house. Quite a few volunteered to go to Haines to attend the hearing to be held at the Commissioner's Office at 10 a.m. January 24, 1920.

January 20, Tuesday: Fifteen below zero. Another piece of water pipe gave way. I turned the stove around and made shorter connection. Walked up to the head of water works and cleaned out the strainer again. Mr. Carr's feet are well enough to care of the cow. Did some writing and visiting in the village.

January 21, Wednesday: Still very cold. Pipes in good shape this morning. I inspected the whole system throughout the town. Cut another load of wood below the 21 mile post. We keep fire in the heater every night. Prayer meeting tonight but only a few out it is so cold. Frank White gave us a fine load of wood.

January 22, Thursday: Twenty-one below zero last night. but we are comfortable in the house and it is beautiful outside. Spent day writing letters to George H., Dr. Condit, Rev. Bruce, Standard Motor Co., Valentine, Rev. Gladfelter, Com. Hirschman. Inspected water system. Made many visits in the village. For some reason at 8 o'clock last night the temperature went up to 10 above zero.

January 23, Friday: Fine weather but down again to 12 below zero. Most of the men have gone to Haines this morning to attend the hearing. Very few dogs left in town. Cut wood, called on a number of people. Milked both this morning and evening. Mr. Carr has gone to Haines again.

January 24, Saturday: Twenty-four below zero this morning, coldest so far this winter. Cut a load of maple. Find it as good as birch for the kitchen stove and I can get it back of the house without the horse. Cleaned up church and woodshed. Everything ready for Sunday.

January 25, Sunday: Milked cow and built fire in church. Quite a number at service but a number of the men still at Haines. Mr. Carr returned with the mail. The hearing about the Council went off in fine shape. Fire alarm sounded at church service. Fire at Postjohnnie's home. Little damage.

January 27, Tuesday: Called on old folks at smoke house. She is so sick so Mr. Carr went to see what medicine was needed. Made arrangements

Klukwan

with Sam R. Johnson to start for Porcupine next Thursday morning.

January 29, Thursday: Left Klukwan at 6 a.m. with Sam R. Johnson and his team of five dogs. Went through Glacier Creek. Did not find the man there but on returning to Porcupine obtained the required information. Counted the people in that large town and stayed at Mr. McGraw's all night. Mr. McGraw provided very good meals at one dollar each.

January 30, Friday: Got up at five. After breakfast started at 7 a.m. Made good run all the way. The woods were beautiful, four feet of snow on the level; at Porcupine, six feet and at Glacier Creek and at different points on the road, five, four, and six feet deep. Good trail all the way. The old lady that lived in the smoke house died this morning at four o'clock. A collection was taken up at the Frog House this afternoon to pay for the coffin, eight dollars and fifty cents. Mr. Carr took a picture of our outfit when we returned. Esten Carr returned from Haines this evening. No mail. Boat did not arrive.

January 3l, Saturday: Conducted funeral service for Gus Klaney's Aunt. Arranged for meeting to nominate candidates for Council. Charles Kladoo gave a sled load of wood to the church.

Cut more wood and visited homes.

February 3, Tuesday: Attended the caucus at the Frog House to nominate candidates for the Council. Mr. Billie Wilson was chairman, Sam R. Johnson secretary. Sam Fox and Mike Ka-dan-a-ha tried to hold meeting back.

February 4, Wednesday: Took the census of a large part of Klukwan this afternoon and held prayer meeting this morning. This morning the feed pipe to the toilet began to leak and I had some trouble in getting it fixed.

February 5, Thursday: Fine in the woods on snow shoes but hard sledding. Took census again this afternoon. Hope to finish tomorrow.

February 6, Friday: Real warm this morning. Seven inches of new snow. A number of slides came down the mountain. Cut some wood for the house. Got a load of maple from the woods. I also split up a couple of blocks of wood for Mrs. Paddie. I still have my census papers and report to finish. I did a little work on it this afternoon and also tried to make peace between Silas Koowhatch and his wife. They are a cranky old pair.

Continued to cut wood, visit people in the village. Charlie Kladoo

Klukwan

brought another sled load of wood.

February 10, Tuesday: Spent most of the day in the school house as it was Election day and Mr. Carr and myself had our hands full. The following men were elected as councilmen and after dinner given by Mr. and Mrs. Carr they organized and elected their own officers: William Johnson, Sr., Mayor; John Benson, Judge; Sam Johnson, secretary; Billie Wilson, treasurer; Gus Klaney and Billie Johnson, marshals; John Willard, Dan Kotzek, Frank White, Jim King, George Willard and Joseph Allen, council members.

February 12, Thursday: Spent yesterday and this morning trying to get water works running. Decorated church and cleaned it up as the Council asked me to administer the oath of office in the church. The people did not turn out well but I believe it was because they did not fully understand. The Council were there. We sang America. Mr. Carr gave a very fine little speech. The Oath was administered and the Council have gone to work.

February 13, Friday: Took Prince out and hauled a load of wood from 21 mile. We are all troubled about the water works. We can't find a leak but there is very little pressure. The Council gave a party to the town this evening and the spirit shown by all was very fine. Mrs. Beck held a meeting of the women and it was very well attended.

February 15, Sunday: Very good attendance at services. Tom Kotzek and his brother had trouble over a lamp. He is to be tried tomorrow by the Council

February 16, Monday: Tom Kotzek was fined fifteen dollars this morning. He paid it. Old John Eshon, the shaman, was fined twenty dollars for kicking his grandson and neglecting his helpless daughter. Now I hear the people are objecting to the tax on dogs but I guess it will come out all right. There is always something to keep the people worked up but it is good for them. Sam R. Johnson, secretary of the Council, called me down to a meeting of the Council at John Benson's house. Mrs. Kadenaha and Dan Hotch asked the council to reduce the dog tax to $1.00 but the Council decided to collect $1.50 for each dog.

February 18, Wednesday: Water was found coming up in the middle of the road in front of Mayor Johnson's house. We worked all day but the ground was frozen so hard we did not get to the leak and quit at 5 p.m.

February 19, Thursday: Turned off the water and found a plug had blown

Klukwan

out. All fixed before noon. Whole system now in good shape. Jack Lea's little girl died. I went to the house and had prayers with them all.

February 20, Friday: Worked all day building a coffin. We made it with round corners and that took a great deal of time. The lumber was full of knots and hard to work up.

February 21, Saturday: Fourteen above zero. Spent good part of day getting ready for Sunday. Held funeral for Jack Lea's daughter at 3 p.m. Could not get the grave ready before that because the ground was frozen so hard and deep.

February 23, Monday: Attended basket social in the evening at the Clancey house. Mr. Carr sold the baskets. They came to $125. Mr. and Mrs. Miller came over from the other side of the river. Mrs. Carr's schoolchildren gave a very good entertainment.

February 27, Friday: Put new water back in stove yesterday. Mr. Jim King called with Dalton Postjohnnie to talk about (Dalton's) getting married. They (Dalton and Lillie) have their license. Charlie Jackson's little boy 4 years old died in Haines yesterday. The body arrived at Frank White's house at three. I have just been down to hold prayer with the friends.

March 1, Monday: We were awakened at 3 a.m. by the ringing of the church bell. The old man in Klaney's house, Jack Williams, had just died. I dressed and called at the house. We were ready for the (Charlie-Postjohnnie) wedding, fire in the church stove and all, when it was decided to put it off until after the funeral.

March 2, Tuesday: The men dug the grave and the funeral was held at twelve. At two p.m. Dalton Postjohnnie and Lillie Charlie were married in the church. The band played and Mrs. Charlie King and Gus Klaney marched in with the couple. At five the dinner was served at the Frog House. The whole town was there, dancing until a late hour.

March 4, Thursday: Read "Man without a Country" last night. Cleaned the chimney and worked about the house today getting ready to move. Inspected the whole water system. All in good shape.

March 7, Sunday: The old Indian doctor John Eshon asked me to cut his hair.

March 8, Monday: Called at several houses and cut the doctor's hair. He went through a great performance before he let me cut it. The Council are shooting dogs today that are without dog tags. They have tagged to

Klukwan

date more than 100 dogs at $2.50 a piece. [No explanation for the higher fee] Hired a young fellow from Haines to do the shooting.

March 10, Wednesday: Number of cases of flu. [Probably an influenza outbreak from the epidemic of 1918 that affected people the world over.] The Council quarantined the town. Mr. Carr the teacher took charge of the medicine and I helped. All others were kept out of the houses.

March 11, Thursday: Many more sick and we are both very busy.

March 12, Friday: People getting sick all the time. Jimmie Johns seems to be the worst. Sent Sam Fox to Haines for supplies and mail.

March 13, Saturday: Thirty-six down. Sam Fox did not return.

March 14, Sunday: Mr. Carr sick. Esten [his brother] came up and asked me to take charge of the sick and milk the cow. Forty-five sick in the village. No church services today. At seven-thirty John Williams house burned to the ground. Five other patients turned out in the snow. George Klaney will start for Haines early in the morning to take the news and find out what has become of Sam Fox.

March 15, Monday: Fifty sick. I have it all to myself. Both teachers sick. The Council are doing fine work and are a great help enforcing regulations, getting wood for the sick folks, and doing all they can.

March 16, Tuesday: Sam and Gus returned with supplies. Sam had been waiting for the steamer from Juneau. Brought word there were three nurses in Haines. Mrs. Carr sent down a dog team to see if one of the nurses would come up. John Willard and Tommy Kotzek went down. Old Mrs. Emma Edwards died today. She was quite old and had been ill for a long time. Jimmie Johns in the same house died this evening at ten. He died holding my hand. He also had been sick for over a year, 22 years of age.

March 17, Wednesday: Sixty cases this morning. I called on each personally to see that they take their pills and salts. Tommy Kotzek returned with the nurse Miss Leroy. After supper we went around to see the worst cases.

March 18, Thursday: No new cases, most recovering. Buried Mrs. Edwards at one o'clock. Walked up to Wells. Mrs. Donnelly and her children are sick. Buried Jimmie Johns at five o'clock.

March 19, Friday: Called at all the houses this morning. Packed five boxes.

March 20, Saturday: Cut wood for Sunday and since there were so many

Klukwan

sick and there would be no services, I planned to rest a bit on the sabbath. But Dr. Kirby and a teacher from Douglas, Mrs. Holman, arrived and we had to take care of the doctor. They also brought up the body of John James.

March 21, Sunday: John James was buried at 2 p.m. from the old tribal house of Chief Yealthcock. What with visiting the sick folks, milking, and feeding the horse and cow, I did not spend much time resting. The people like Mrs. Leroy the nurse and all feel she is helping them.

March 22, Monday: Can't say much for the doctor and the people have no faith in him. Sam R. Johnson seems to be in bad shape. I visited all the sick. Keeps me busy.

March 23, Tuesday: Dr. Kirby says the people are not very sick and got Harry Lead to take Mrs. Holman and himself down to Haines. Sam Johnson is much worse. I called several times at the house. At seven I went to the school house and told the nurse I did not think he would live. We went up to see him and he was quite hopeful. I came home and rested an hour and a half and when I went back at ten he was just breathing his last. He died holding my hand. James King and I washed and dressed him. We left him in his own house but moved the family out. I retired at midnight.

March 24, Wednesday: There seemed to be a little trouble over who should have charge of Sam's funeral. It seems settled however and a coffin was built but word was sent to Haines, Jimmie Anderson making the trip to Haines and back the same day on foot. John Abbot arrived at ten with another coffin and Miss Brown a nurse from the hospital at Haines. The ground was frozen so hard it took all day to dig the grave. Two skulls of former slaves were dug up but no attention was paid to them. The body was buried at 6:30 p.m.

March 25, Thursday: The Council appointed John D. Ward to fill the vacancy caused by the death of Sam Johnson.

March 26, Friday: Mary Shorty very sick. Lost her baby but we hope she will recover. Charlie Kotlawah very sick.

March 27, Saturday: Mary seems a little better. Charlie Kotlawah showed some improvement. Joe King and Joe Johnson both very much better.

March 28, Sunday: Held service this morning. About 40 present. Mr. Carr and the two nurses attended. Mrs. Beck and I visited all the sick this evening.

Klukwan

March 29, Monday: Got up at 5:30. Sorted out my papers and got my trunk ready to pack. Called at Harry Lea's house to see Mary. She seemed much better and called me back to have prayers with her. Made three trips to cut wood. Mary died this afternoon.

March 30, Tuesday: Spent the day visiting and packing. Supper with teachers. Mail arrived. Good news from the boy. Travel check from the Board. $58 allowed for my census work. The river has frozen over and we don't know when we can get out.

The journal ends at this point. The only indication in the journal that the Becks would be leaving is the comment on March 30 that he is packing. They had evidently mentioned to Kosseyia that they would be going to Hoonah, for a March 9, 1920, letter to them said she would send the next letters to Hoonah. In the same letter she said that the scarf for her dad [probably for his birthday—March 29] was not yet ready. In other letters she mentioned items that she had made as gifts for her parents. By this time she was working in New York.

HOONAH AGAIN

Dr. Condit must have posted the Becks to Hoonah, but there is little on record of their arrival and early days there in 1920. Letters suggest, though, that Reverend Beck attacked his new duty with his usual vigor and enthusiasm and he again succeeded greatly with the natives. However, shortly before their ten-year stay in Hoonah was up, a tragic happening was to invade their lives.

Letters from Kosseyia are practically nonexistent during the early twenties; there were none at all between 1919 and 1924, during which time she would have become engaged and have married Albert Duff. Correspondence, which had been frequent before and after that time, probably continued to be so, but had been lost.

In June 1923 George, almost 21 then, wrote his parents from Ketchikan offering to go to Seattle to help his Dad bring up one of the boats and he seemed eager to spend time working with his father. Though he had been out of high school and working full time for a year he did not have money for a ticket and was hoping the Home Missions Board would supply one. There is also a copy of an invitation to Kosseyia's wedding on March 10, 1923, but there is no indication that the Becks attended. A letter in June 1924 told of the birth of their first child Wayne on May 9 of that year, ten days before Kosseyia's mother's birthday.

An occasional notice in the Verstovian mentions the Becks, like one in November 1921 reporting that they and Reverend David Waggoner of Juneau accompanied S. Hall Young, the Board's oldest living missionary to Alaska, in the Lois on his visit to Sitka during the summer. And various bills hint at his moving about. A bill dated September 6, 1922, from the Frye Hotel where Reverend Beck always stopped in Seattle suggests that he was in that city at the time, and a September 27 bill for work done on the Lois from Bertleson Boiler Repair in Juneau suggests he also visited there on the Lois.

But it is mainly through letters between Mr. Beck and the Board of Home Missions dating from 1922 that the work of those early days in Hoonah is known. Several communications between Mr. Beck and Varian Banks, Home Missions Board Treasurer, deal first with the building of a manse in Hoonah and also the building of a new boat, the Princeton.

Hoonah Again

Dear Mr. Beck,

As soon as I could get to it, after getting to my desk, I made application to the Board of Church Erection for a grant of $5,355 from the Manse Fund to erect your new home at Hoonah. I received a reply from Dr. Wylie stating that he cannot encourage me to hope for an appropriation of anything like that amount as the Manse Fund is heavily over appropriated and the Board has been compelled to limit their loans from this fund. Dr. Wylie asks, "What will become of the old manse upon which we made a grant of $500 in 1913?" Now I am up against this question which in my own mind I am unable to answer, namely: What is to be done with your present manse? Is it a total loss?

In this stressful financial time of the Board, it is not going to be an easy matter to secure any satisfactory sum with which to provide you with a new house and especially when it is known that the present building will then be of no practicable value to the Home Missions. I realize that no part of this question arose on your own initiation and that not even in the most indirect manner did you ask for a new building. I believe however that from the representations made from Mr. Waggoner you should have a new home but I feel that the effort would be greatly helped if we can realize something on your present building as above stated. Will you write me frankly about this whole matter as I have advised Dr. Wylie of the Board of Erection that I would write you and await your reply before taking this matter up with him further.

Brother Keeler has sent me a good letter concerning the result of the luncheon and thought it was more than worthwhile for you and Brother Waggoner to run down to the Coast to see to this boat matter and after your conference with Mr. Cunningham return to Hoonah loaded with data. I believe the boat is assured and I sincerely hope that the Princeton will soon become a thing of beauty and a joy forever. I hope you and your good wife are enjoying good health resulting from a change in climate.

Very cordially yours,   (signed) Varian Banks

A letter dated September 25, 1922, included a check in payment for repairs to the Lois and discussed property matters.

Hoonah Again

The recommendations regarding the property matters at Sitka, Hoonah, and Haines, according to the understanding arrived at during that fine conference we had at Mr. Waggoner's home, were presented to our executive council and they heartily approved the presentation of same to our Finance Committee as their recommendations. I therefore hope that soon after the next meeting of our Board to be held on the 5th approximately, I will have the pleasure of writing you that the Board has officially and definitely taken the action that you have so long desired.

Mr. Beck's answer to both letters was dated October 27, 1922:

My dear Mr. Banks:

Neither Mrs. Beck or myself believe a five or six thousand dollar house is needed at this station. It is nice to have standardized houses on all the fields but it really would be better to have a small cottage here for it will be a long time before a minister with a large family could live in Hoonah because he could not educate his children. We have no way of telling how long we shall stay but do not look forward with a great deal of pleasure of caring for a large house. We do feel however that a good lighting plant is very essential and we must get it in some way. I will enclose a catalog with the plant we really need (Model # 866). The one plant will light the church as well as the house and will be a great lever to pry these people out of the rut they are in. I know the old time missionaries never asked for all these things and neither have we for thirty years. But times have changed and we need them now to meet changed conditions.

Now Mr. Banks we want the work of the Lord to prosper in this part of the world. We don't want house, boat, or lighting plant unless it is for the best interest of His service. We want a boat that is a bit longer and wider than the Lois that she may keep at sea in all weather and carry the gospel to all the people of Southeastern Alaska all the year round. We have only half done the work so far and now is the time to finish what we have begun. Mrs. Beck and I have spent so much time running the ship we have not had time enough to preach the Word. You know all this but I have just written it down on paper for it sort of relieves the pressure.

Hoonah Again

As always, Mr. Beck is encouraging self-reliance and enterprise among the natives.

> *The men who built the two model cottages on the mission ground harvested about ten sacks of potatoes in each of their little plots. I have ordered a drag saw for one of them and they will saw wood for sale. Keep it on hand for those who will buy. I have never been able to get anyone to do this before. They had to see the money in sight before and for that reason it was impossible to buy dry wood.*
>
> *Yesterday's mail brought a request from Mr. Waggoner that I take the Lois to Juneau next month and carry Dr. Young and himself to Angoon to organize the new church there then take lumber to Kake to put the L.A. Lindsley in shape to tow to Seattle. The latter part of March I must take all the Presbytery to Bayview (round trip being 400 miles) to the spring meeting of Presbytery. How it will be possible to build that manse is more than I can see.*
>
> *I don't think a six thousand dollar house is needed here. We are willing to make any sacrifice for the good of the service as we have done for so long. I sometimes feel the missionaries are losing the importance of sacrifice in their work. We are hoping to develop our boat work that we can live on the little ship all year round. In that case, someone else will live here.*
>
> *We have all the fittings for a first class bathroom. There is no provision for such a room in the plans sent. We feel it will be much better to live on in the old building until such time as it will be possible to erect an adequate manse.*
>
> *Trusting you will understand me in this matter and know that we are truly grateful for all the blessings received and wishing the very best things for the year before you, I remain*
>   *Most cordially yours, (Signed George J. Beck)*

A reply to this letter from Mr. Banks, dated December 11, 1922, had some good news in regard to building the manse.

> *Dear Mr. Beck,*
> *You will recall that Mr. Keeler at the conference we had in Seattle concerning the boat proposition and in connection with the proposed*

Hoonah Again

new manse at Hoonah suggested that he might be able to get one of his friends in the lumber business to either sell the required amount of lumber for the new building at a very low price or possibly to donate it. The man he referred to was Mr. A.G. Hansen.

Mr. Keeler has submitted a definite proposition which he has received from Mr. Hansen, which will largely decrease the cost of the proposed new manse building at Hoonah. I am just making this additional word of explanation that you may understand what relation to this matter Mr. Hansen has and that he has shown a generous desire to cooperate effectively in supplying the new manse building.

I would suggest that in harmony with my letter of even date enclosed, when writing Mr. Keeler, you send me a carbon copy giving your reaction on the proposed building.

I think there is no question but that we can secure the required amount from the Board Church Erection.

Sincerely yours,   (Signed) Varian Banks, Treasurer

Hoonah: Cannery, School, Church, Manse.

Hoonah Again

Another letter from Mr. Banks also dated December 11, 1922, spelled out details of the proposed new manse, which was to be a 24' x 26' house with two-bedrooms, a living room and a kitchen. Before accepting "the very generous proposal of Mr. Hansen" for lumber, Mr. Banks wanted Mr. Beck to look over the plans and be sure it was suitable for present and future needs. "We want at this time to be well assured that a tight, warm building is erected so that the occupants may be well protected against the rigorous winter climate." He was instructed to reply directly to Mr. Keeler. Then Mr. Banks asked, "If the lumber and all material required for the new manse building is sent up during February, can you secure the right kind of help to put up the building in time for use by the first or middle of May? Maybe this is expecting too much."

In a letter dated January 13, from Mr. Banks, referring to a note that Mr. Beck had written concerning the manse, cautioned him that a large meeting place might not be acceptable to the Board.

> *The information you have given me makes it very clear that the new manse building should provide for something more than living and sleeping quarters and a bathroom. Therefore I will submit the matter anew to Mr. Keeler asking that he confer with Mr. Hansen, the lumber man, as to what lumber for a larger building will cost, the plans for which shall provide for a bathroom, office, and for a room sufficiently large to be used for small assemblies. The latter item we may not be able to provide to as full an extent as you would wish. . .Would not a room to permit 15 or 20 be sufficiently large, and when larger numbers are expected could not the church be used?*

A letter from Mr. Banks dated January 12 dealt with the plots Mr. Beck suggested they provide the natives.

> *I am awaiting, at your convenience, the photographs of the buildings already erected by the natives on the Board's land in Hoonah. I am hoping that from what I have already said to you, there will accompany these photographs as strong a presentation as you can make in support of the proposition to convey to the natives already having erected houses, and to those who desire to do so, deeds to the*

Hoonah Again

plots of ground which they may select with your approval.

In presenting this matter to the Board, I stated that the men who have already erected houses on the Board's land are citizens of the United States. They are unable to obtain land elsewhere in Hoonah on which to erect their homes. They recognize that the Board obtained the land for the benefit of the native Indians. . . . . The missionary of the Board having induced them to give up their former way of living in communal houses would naturally expect the Board to be consistent with its teachings by affording these natives an opportunity, through the only outlet available, to erect houses on land among the native people. . .

Mr. Banks brought up the point that the Board might make: If the Indians were able to pay for a house why wouldn't they be able to pay for the land rather than ask for it free? He asked for his help with an answer to that one.

On a lighter note are several letters from S. Hall Young that show a certain camaraderie between him and George J. Beck. In a letter, dated September 27, 1921, Dr. Young, 74 at the time, wrote, "I am flat on my back with lumbago and dictating this letter from that position. Have been afflicted in this way for two weeks. Am somewhat better and hope to be about in a few days. . . .The more I think of the splendid trip I had with you and Mrs. Beck in the Lois, the more it stands out as one of the great events in my life." He promised to send pictures he took on the trip.

Dr. Young reported that he had been able to secure a raise from the Home Board for the ministers "on the strength of your report" but was not sure he would be able to get funding for some project asked for by Mr. Beck [possibly repairs for the Lois], as the Board was short of funds and had had to take out loans for other promised undertakings. He did add however, "I believe that I can get Mr. Childs to endow the Lois and that the Board will appoint you as pastor-evangelist and grant you the theological students to be put in training. . . .. I intend to make appeals before the churches the coming winter for all that is necessary in the boat line to make the work of the missionaries successful."

A letter from Dr. Young dated February 28, 1922, declared, "I am glad you take disappointments so philosophically. Like you, I hope that we

Hoonah Again

will get the $1100 this year, and so be enabled to have the Lois do the full work of an evangelist. I have not yet received the $500 from Mr. Childs but am looking forward to it." A good minister was needed at Kake, and Reverend Young asked, "Why could you not be sounding Paul White as to whether he would be willing to devote the time and study necessary to prepare himself thoroughly as a native minister. We need to be rustling them up if we are going to carry out our plan of evangelism." He then discussed several possible candidates for the job of apprentice on the Lois and ended by thanking Mr. Beck for a picture of himself to be used in a booklet.

The booklet referred to was one put out by the Board of Home Missions about "The Trail Blazers of Today" in the Presbyterian missions. Each of the ministers included was asked to state his job, to let the Board know what it could do to help, to give words of encouragement for young men in the seminary. George J. Beck told of his evangelistic work on the Lois and asked for "a boat large enough to weather all storms and send out with it a real red-blooded doctor who will be willing to do his share of the work on board as well as minister to the needy ones in a material and spiritual way." Then in answer to the question posed by the booklet, "Is there a man's job in the Home Mission Field?" he assured the young seminarians that there was. "Would you call it a man's job to lead five hundred native people in their joys and sorrows, in politics, business, and religion? To stand watch in the wheelhouse all the way round the clock? To fight great waves, ice, rocks, fogs, darkness? To build coffins, dig graves, visit the sick, put down riots? If there is anything else needed to make up a man's job, it can be found on the Home Mission field."

"I like my job," he added, "I find in it the joy of beholding changed lives."

In a letter of March 2, 1923, Dr. Young, who had returned to Alaska as chaplain to the Legislature in Juneau, wrote, "Winterberger will be down here about the fifteenth. You and he and I could live very handily and take turns cooking. He is going to stop with me and we might rig up a davenport for you, that is If Mrs. Beck does not come with you. Please let me know if you have any other arrangements. My latch string is out for you."

The same letter informed Mr. Beck that Doctor Young had received the $500 from Mr. Child but was still expecting $600 from the Board for ex-

Hoonah Again

penses in running the Lois. It ended, "You did not tell me when you expect to come to Juneau. If you sleep on board the Lois you can take a lot of meals with Winterberger and me at my house." But in a letter two weeks later Dr. Young mentioned that he and Winterberger were at his house, having fun teaching each other how to cook, which suggests that Reverend Beck had been unable to be with them. Young was going to Ketchikan the following week, however, and would stay until Beck got there.

In a letter dated June 7, 1923, Dr. Young stated that Mr. Story would be needed as minister at Skagway for the summer since there were so many tourists, many of them Presbyterian. The people at Petersburg had submitted a petition signed by 44 people for a Presbyterian church there. He also reported that Dorothy Kleinschmidt, a great grandniece of Dr. Lindsley, would break the bottle of "Elixir Vitae" on the bow of the A.L.Lindsley for its dedication. Previously a February 1923 letter from Mr. Banks had announced that there was money for renovating that boat, which upon completion would be used at Kake. Arrangements were to have been made immediately for towing the hull south so that the work could be completed by May 15, 1923. Evidently work had gone according to schedule.

During this period the Verstovian reported an event of July 22, 1923, as a most memorable day in its history. "On that day President Warren Harding, President of the United States, honored this school, and the Board which sustains it, by his presence and his approval." President Harding delivered the sermon that Sunday in the Tlingit Presbyterian Church in Sitka. It was his last attendance at public worship, as he was to die a short time afterwards.

In a reply to comments made in a letter from Varian Banks, Reverend Beck wrote in November 1923 that the natives should not be expected to pay for the land being given them by the Home Missions Board, because they had tilled that land before whites arrived and because white men do not pay for land but are granted it upon staking a claim.

A church journal fragment for November 1923 noted that 160 attended morning services in Hoonah on Sunday, November 18. Monday: "Spent the day laying the floor in the attic and moving things from old house" and Tuesday "Spent the day making and putting up shelves in the office." Evidently the new manse was finished. By November 26 the men of the village were painting the new hall and digging for a new dam. On Wednesday

Hoonah Again

November 28 a congregational meeting was held and officers elected: Sarah Osborne and Louie Houston, Elders; William Sheakley and John Fawsette, Deacons. Appointed to the church committee were Mrs. Oscar Williams, Mrs. George Dawson, Mrs. Archie Lawrence, and Mrs. George Wallace. On Thursday, November 29, all attended Thanksgiving dinner in the new hall. In the same book with the journal fragments were some Tlingit phrases with their English translations, as "Come to church" and "Are you coming to my home?"

In February of 1924 Reverend Beck had a frightening experience that could have been tragic; an explosion destroyed the Lois and nearly took his life. He was lucky to have escaped with severe burns. When the natives saw him emerge from the wreckage, white from head to toe from flour that had filled the air from the explosion, they thought they were witnessing his spirit leaving his body. Again it was his own words that dramatized the event as he described it in detail in a letter on March 1924 to Varian Banks.

> *On the afternoon of February 20, an ice floe came down the bay. It was two hundred feet long by thirty feet wide and three or four inches thick—very large for this bay. One end struck the point of Grove Island and the other caught the Lois, forcing her ashore. I chopped ice for three hours and finally freed her, but the outgoing tide left her high and dry.*
>
> *It was prayer meeting night and I had just talked to the natives from Acts, Chapter 26, verses 28 and 29. A few minutes later when the explosion and fire took place, the natives believed that I was dead and that those had been my last words.*
>
> *It was a dark night. A southeaster was blowing, so after church I took my lantern and pulled over to see if all was well with the boat. She was lying on her side almost ready to float as the tide was coming in. I entered the main cabin and passed through the wheelhouse and down into the engine room. I walked to the far end of the engine and picked up my blow torch, which had been overturned when the boat listed. As I stooped to pick it up, there came a blinding flash. That is all I know. I did not hear the explosion that shook every house in town. The whole room was one mass of red flame. I did not feel it, but decided to get out if possible. I reached for the ladder but*

Hoonah Again

found only a mass of wreckage. Climbing over it, I felt for the wheelhouse door. Not finding it, I realized my eyes were closed and on opening them I found myself standing on the edge of the boat.

The wheelhouse, decks, cabin and steel rigging were all clear of the ship and lying on the ice on the opposite side. The hull itself was a mass of flame fifty feet high. As the fire raged on one side of me and the black water filled with ice was on the other, I stood on the rail only a few inches wide. It seemed some great power was guiding me, for a clear voice said, "Don't jump. It will be bad for your burns."

I walked the rail nearly forty feet between the fire and the deep sea. Then I dropped off the stern onto the floating ice and made shore without wetting my feet. To the people on shore it looked as if I was walking in the fire, and as I dropped over the stern they thought I had dropped into it. They gave me up then, but were determined to recover my body at all costs. The women (God bless them) went over to help and comfort Mrs. Beck, and by the light of the fire I saw the little boats putting out from all points.

A gas boat with twenty men on board sailed right up to the wreck, determined to pull her into deeper water, but then they heard me call to keep clear of her. I was afraid of another explosion. Nothing could be done and as far as the boat was concerned, she was lost from the first moment. I can only suppose that one or both of the main feed pipes had broken off and a large quantity of gasoline had emptied into the bilge and the boat filled with gas.

I shall never forget my trip from the dock to the house. The people did not know I was burned and wanted to shake hands with me. I believe at least two hundred people touched me and the air was filled with exclamations of "Praise God" and "The Lord be praised." The nurse gave me first aid. I was burned about the face. My eyebrows and eye lashes were gone. The rims of my glasses were partly melted. My face was swollen and the next day my eyes were completely closed. My eyesight was not impaired.

The natives with four gas boats raised the hull, which was split wide open down to the keel. All this loss is a great grief to me. It will make a great difference in my work this summer, but the good Lord knows.

Hoonah Again

The February 24, 1924 Sitka Alaskan reported the accident: "The Reverend George J. Beck was burned about the face and hands but received no permanent injuries when the Presbyterian mission boat Lois blew up and burned here [Hoonah] last night. The boat, owned by Board of Presbyterian Missions, is a total loss with the value placed at $15,000. It had operated in the waters of Southeastern Alaska for the past twelve years."

In addition to his taking care of the Mission boat and building a manse in Hoonah, Mr. Beck devised a plan for developing agriculture among the natives. Several letters between August 1925 and January 1926 concerned this proposed agricultural project. On August 1, he wrote the Women's Home Board, saying the women "have been responsible to a large extent for the fact that high school graduates are not uncommon among our native people . . . . . (and) that citizenship is an established fact, and the right to hold property, transact business and enjoy all other privileges in this grand country of ours is secured to all Alaskans." He requested their support for his plan to "let every native take up five acres of government land, clear it, raise all the vegetables, chickens, and eggs for his family and sell the rest," in order to give them a steady source of food and income. The Governor and Forestry Service approved his plan but said, "The natives won't do it." Mr. Beck thought otherwise.

"To start this work we should have a very small portable sawmill that will cost no more than $700. I have seen the machine we want; two men can operate it and move it from tract to tract. . . a Fordson tractor that will cost in Juneau $669.50, which will not only plow, harrow and make roads but will furnish the power to run the saw mill and shingle mill. The two mills, hoist with 500 feet of cable, plow, blocks and freight should bring the total cost to no more than $3,000." The Women's Board was enthusiastic about the program, but cited the Home Board's $500,000 debt to warn him of possible refusal. On September 21 a letter from the Home Board Division of schools and Hospitals suggested that Reverend Beck submit his request to the Division of Church Extension and Missions, and the answer there was that he would have to wait. A letter from a minister in Philadelphia who had been trying to help find an agriculturist for the project reported that a qualified young man had stepped forward but could not afford to go as a volunteer. So the Board sent him to Puerto Rico as groundskeeper. "He could hardly have been sent farther away from Alaska

Hoonah Again

than that, could he?" the minister asked. On November 7, 1925, Reverend Beck wrote in reply to a request for information from Mr. E. R. Deffenbaugh of California outlining the need for and feasibility of the same project.

By 1925 the project attracted an enthusiastic job applicant. On October 12, J.R. Armbruster wrote regarding an article he had read in the Presbyterian Magazine and listed his qualifications as a possible agriculturist. "I am free to come to your assistance if deemed advisable financially and otherwise." The young man was the answer to Mr. Beck's hopes and he replied with pictures and a desire to see him. Hopes for funding rose when Mr. Armbruster notified Mr. Beck on November 27 that the agricultural project had been introduced to the Board. But again disappointment came with a January 7 letter from Mr. Armbruster saying that the project had not been included in the 1925-26 budget. Reverend Beck sent all the letters to the Missions Committee and became resigned to putting the project on hold.

Word of the death of his old friend and mentor S. Hall Young in September of 1927 brought sadness to the Becks. An article in the October 27, 1927, Verstovian, noting his death on September 2, called Dr. Young "the last of that notable band, the 'old guard' of pioneer missionaries, which includes Sheldon Jackson, Mrs. A. R. MacFarland, John Brady, and Alonzo E. Austin. Talented by nature, versatile in attainment and blessed with a long life of opportunity and service, he was in many respects the most noted of them all." Dr. Young had gone to Wrangell in 1878 and in 1879 organized the church there. Within a short time he had established missions throughout Southeast Alaska and at Skagway, Fairbanks, Eagle, Teller, and Dawson, most of which became full fledged churches afterwards. The article rated Dr. Young's gift of friendship as his most endearing quality and his eternal optimism as his second.

S. Hall Young's exuberant enthusiasm and adventurous spirit are shown in his scaling glaciers and performing other hair-raising feats, which he recorded in his book, ALASKA DAYS WITH JOHN MUIR. An unfinished poem found in Dr. Young's pocket when he was struck down and killed in a streetcar accident also expresses his love of an active life:

Hoonah Again

Let me die working,
Still tackling plans unfinished, tasks undone;
Clear to its end, may my race be run,
No laggard steps, no faltering, no shirking
Let me die working.

His wife, Fannie Kellogg Young, the first teacher at what was to become Sheldon Jackson School, had died in 1915.

In 1928 there were further letters from George Herbert and Kosseyia. Young George wrote his parents on January 25, telling of various happenings in Ketchikan. Buddy (George Lauren), who had been born in 1925 and was now three and a half, could pick out certain letters from the newspaper and was full of life, on the go all the time. George was planning to take him in to have his tonsils out.

Kosseyia's letters at that time dealt with all kinds of news: the health of her parents and children, the children's antics, business, and the new house they were planning. In February of 1928 she wrote mentioning that her husband Albert's mother was very ill and not expected to live. Wayne had had a tonsillectomy and was slow to recover. She was concerned about her own mother's health and urged her to see a doctor. Three letters in June of 1928 told of the birth of the new baby Joan, who she reported was doing well and gaining weight. Wayne had been in bed with the measles for ten days but was getting better. She asked how the agricultural business was going. In July they had entertained some business associates of Alfred, who worked for a mimeograph company, and had gone to a movie with them.

In August she mentioned that Alfred Chace, then 12 years older than when they were growing up together, was spending some time with them. At first she was annoyed by his know-it-all attitude, but then conceded he was really very nice, just a little young for his years. He was selling used cars, after his parents had discouraged him from pursuing a flying career. By November 7 she was talking of the new house they were having built in Malverne on Long Island, New York. By February they had moved in and she described the house in detail for them. The progress and amusing antics of the children were recounted in most of her letters.

In the meantime, the idea for Mr. Beck's agricultural project had been

Hoonah Again

kept alive. In reply to requests to various businesses for funds, a letter dated August 14, 1928, from Archie Shiels of Pacific American Fisheries told him to talk over his plan with Mr. Faulkner in Juneau, who had authority to contribute something to the [agricultural] cause if he found it feasible. Then in a letter dated December 1, 1928, to Reverend Diven, Chairman of the Alaska Presbytery, Mr. Beck referred to a decision he had to make on whether he should return to Sitka or stay at Hoonah. He would have dearly loved to return to his beloved Sitka but he felt he should stay with the agricultural project at Hoonah. He had been overwhelmed by the treatment he received from the people of Sitka when he attended the ANB convention there. "The Alaska Native Brotherhood insisted on my attending all sessions of the convention even those meetings closed to all but delegates or members of the Grand Camp. I did not mention the matter of going back to Sitka to any one there until Ralph Young [the young man for whom he had surveyed the Chichagof mine claim years earlier] brought the matter up himself just before I started home. . . . He told me the people of Sitka were united in wanting us back and were willing to wait for us until we could get our work in shape to turn it over to another man."

His old friend S. Hall Young continued to help him and his agricultural project from the world beyond. A note in an anniversary paper put out by the Board of Home Missions in January of 1928 mentioned that $3,000 had been requested by Mr. Beck of Hoonah from the S. Hall Memorial Fund for agricultural projects. Evidently the money was given, as later communications show that he had purchased some of the machinery.

A letter from Juneau Motors in January of 1929 mentioned receiving Mr. Beck's order for a Fordson tractor and a Hyster winch. In February 1929 Andrew Montgomery wrote from the Home Board in New York rejoicing that the agricultural machinery could be ordered and that more money would be available. A February letter from Juneau Motors said they were glad he had the Hyster winch in running order and that it was performing as promised.

Money also became available at this time for repairs to the A. L. Lindsley, named for the Reverend Aaron L. Lindsley, the Portland Presbyterian minister, who from 1879 until his death in 1891 helped in the development of the church in Alaska. Dr. Robert Diven, chairman of the Committee of National Missions in Alaska, on which he served with the reverends Beck

Hoonah Again

and Waggoner, told him to thank Dr. Montgomery for getting the $2,000 for work on the Lindsley. But Dr. Diven was afraid the amount allowed for repairing the Princeton would not be enough.

George H. reported in a letter to his parents on February 13, 1929, that he had seen Reverend Falconer, minister at the Ketchikan Presbyterian church, and hoped to sell him a Radiola 16 radio for the Princeton. George was working for Smith Electric and had been voted into the Gyro Club. Buddy had just turned four. Like Kosseyia, George expressed concern for his mother's health and thought that they should consider giving up their work in Hoonah.

What is known of the folks' relationship with Kosseyia and George is revealed through their children's letters. No letters from the parents to the children are available. Kosseyia's letters were frequent from January through May and reveal that the family was happy and all was well. In January of 1929 she wrote that they had moved into their new house and that Alfred Chace had sent them a lovely set of bookends. She thanked her parents for their gift and the check, which she would spend on something for the house. She was glad that her mother's rheumatism was better. They must have told her about the possibility of going to Sitka, because she wrote, "Sorry you are not going to Sitka, but you know what is best." In February she mentioned that Wayne liked Sunday school and went by himself the last time. Kosseyia was happy that her own weight had dropped to 135. In March they acquired a kitten that had followed them into the house and a puppy that Albert had bought from some children selling them door-to door.

Her April letter told that Wayne had been registered to start school in the fall, at which time he would be five-and-a-half years old. In May she wrote to wish her mother a happy mother's day, saying that she thought of her often each day. She was surprised to hear that Mr. Kirberger, owner of the store at Kake where George had worked when the family lived there, had been married. Wayne, who was eagerly looking forward to the party for his fifth birthday, had suggested to his mother that she start cleaning the house to get ready for it. She was happy to see that the grass seed was starting to come up; when they first moved, she had complained of the mud being tracked in. Albert had given her a Majestic radio—all electric—which they were enjoying immensely. George H. had mentioned in

Hoonah Again

his letters to his folks that he sold that type of radio at work. A letter the following week wished her mother a happy birthday and mentioned that the warm early summer was especially enjoyable as they now lived in the country where the children could play safely away from the dangers of the city. Life was peaceful and pleasant.

Then a month later on June 25, 1929, an alarming letter came from Albert, explaining that Kosseyia had been unable to write because Wayne was very sick and had been diagnosed with infantile paralysis. His playmate Richard Workman had come down with the disease too, and it was believed they had both been exposed at the same time. The doctors felt that the crisis had passed for Wayne the day before and that he was on the mend. There had been no serum available locally, but they had been able to get an eminent specialist in infantile paralysis to come from New York and bring serum with him. They felt the early diagnosis and two injections had helped keep the paralysis from spreading. Wayne's temperature was normal that morning, he was able to move all parts of his body except his right leg, and he was playing with his toys. The doctor thought he would

Bud on His Grandpa's Shoulders by A.L. Lindsley.

Hoonah Again

eventually have a slight limp in the right leg. For twenty-one days nobody but the nurse could go into the room, especially Kosseyia, who had to take care of little Joan. Albert would be writing to them until after the quarantine so that there would be no danger that germs from the letter would infect Buddy, who was with the elder Becks at the time.

Twelve days later came the good news that Wayne was definitely on the mend, but had to be kept in bed another week, a difficult task since he was becoming restless. Kosseyia was taking care of him then, since "all danger of the disease spreading is now passed. But we are taking no chance on account of Joan and are keeping ourselves pretty lysoled." In those days the disease was thought of as a childhood illness.

Then on July 10, 1929, the heart-breaking news was telegraphed from Brooklyn, New York, to the Becks at Hoonah: "Kosseyia passed away suddenly Tuesday. Infantile Paralysis. Funeral Thursday. Will Wire. Wayne okay. Albert." The following day George wired them from Ketchikan: "Wire from Albert this morning that Kosseyia passed away yesterday from infantile paralysis. I wired flowers and offered to take the children. Shock is terrible but is God's will and we must make the best of it. Albert said that letter would follow. Funeral to be Thursday. George."

On July 1, before Kosseyia's death, George had written his parents to tell them that Marge and Buddy were home with them and he was thrilled to have them back. He hoped they had not minded that he had addressed all his letters to Marge while she and Buddy were with them for six weeks, as the letters had been intended for all of them. But that carefree letter was followed on July 11 by a heavy-hearted one, in which he spoke of Kosseyia's sudden death and tried to console his parents. Of course, he himself was numbed by the sudden loss of his sister and was sympathetic toward Albert. "Last fall when I nearly lost Marge, the pain and agony of that time is still fresh in my memory and I can appreciate what poor Albert is going through now. I would like to be with him and share his load."

His attempt to accept the situation reflects the strong religious upbringing he had had. "You two are the grandest parents that God ever gave and I know that this blow will not be too hard for you, knowing you as I do. It is terrible, and is a thing that leaves a scar that never heals, but it is God's way of making us realize we are solely dependent on him. I want to know that you dear Mother and Dad will always remember that your son and his

Hoonah Again

family here in Ketchikan love you dearly, and want to so conduct ourselves that we will be a source of joy to you." He closed by inviting them to visit him and the family in Ketchikan.

Letters poured in from family and friends. Albert was unable to write until July 21, 1929, but his letter gave a riveting account of Kosseyia's brief illness and death.

Dear Mother and Dad,

So much has been crowded into my life in the last month it does not seem real. Of course, you want all the details. I want to give them to you but it is so hard. You will pardon me if I do not delve too deeply. Aunt Lulu [Mr. Beck's sister Elizabeth] wrote me the other day and stated that she had given you the details of the funeral. I am happy for that as I know her explanation of it would be finer than mine.

Words are too inadequate to convey the depths of my feeling and love for Kosseyia. There is a consolation in the fact that there is a higher power than ours which we can turn to for comfort and guidance.

Kosseyia has left her mark behind her: Wayne and Joan, two beautiful, adorable children. It is not necessary to take the doting father's word as every body who comes in contact with them says so. Then Kosseyia was my balance. She helped me more that anyone will ever know. There could not be a better mother or wife than Kosseyia. It seems a shame that such a young life and such a good life should suddenly be taken from this earth. God knows best however and he is caring for Kosseyia and leading her in that finer life which we know is beyond.

Just two weeks ago today, Sunday, Kosseyia was taken sick. She arose in the usual way, put on Joan's bottle, and came into me. Her remark was, "I don't feel well, Albert, will you look after the baby?" She went back to bed and Mrs. Driscoll, the housekeeper and myself took hold of things.

The doctor arrived around ten a.m. His statement was that it looked like summer flu, but due to Wayne's trouble he stated if Kosseyia was not better in the morning he would tap her spine and have it analyzed. At the same time he would give her an injection of infantile

Hoonah Again

> *paralysis serum. On Monday she was not better so Dr. Mehler tapped. Imagine my feelings when the report came back negative. I was so overjoyed I rushed around telling the neighbors.*
>
> *My joy did not last long. A short time after I received the report over the phone, the doctor again came and remarked although the report was negative, the symptoms were there and that he would be back the following day and give Kosseyia the serum. The mean part about infantile paralysis is that the paralysis does not show up for at least three days, or I should say it shows up any time within three days and no one ever knows what part of the body it will strike.*
>
> *Unfortunately in Kosseyia's case it struck the diaphragm. Monday she was uncomfortable and restless. Tuesday up to eleven a.m. she was about the same but about that time the paralysis started to show and her breathing became somewhat heavy. At two o'clock the doctors ordered a pulmotor and oxygen. Thank God Kosseyia lapsed into unconsciousness within half an hour. We used the pulmotor, oxygen, and in between times the nurses, doctors, and I gave her artificial respiration, but to no avail. At eight p.m. Tuesday Kosseyia closed her eyes.*

He then talked of the actions of close relatives, and added:

> *Wayne is doing splendidly. He is up and around but as yet he does not walk or stand up. Within a few days he will do that too. In my next letter I will tell you all about him.*
> *With love from all, (signed) Albert*

Relatives and friends wrote in a state of shock. All of the missionaries Mr. Beck had worked with over the years sent their condolences: the reverends Diven, Waggoner, Falconer, Bromley, Pederson, and Condit; the widow of Governor John Brady. Many of them had witnessed Kosseyia pass from childhood into adulthood and were crushed to think that her young life had been snuffed out so soon. Some had retired to New York and she had visited them there as a young adult. Reverend Austin had died in May of 1927 and his good friend S. Hall Young in September of the same year.

There are no letters or recorded comments from her parents, but the shock and grief at the loss of their only daughter must have been intense.

Hoonah Again

Her letters and pictures—especially one of her ruffling her father's hair as the picture is being taken—show her as fun-loving and high-spirited, which made her early demise harder to fathom. The Becks had witnessed and grieved over the deaths of children and friends and had sustained others in their loss. Now they needed to be comforted.

The letters of condolence were neatly arranged and saved, along with letters Kosseyia had written them over the years. Mr. Beck's co-missionary for so many years, Matilda Paul Tamaree, who had given their daughter the Tlingit name of Kosseyia, shared their grief and yet knew their spiritual strength. She too had lost a daughter, as well as a husband.

My very dear Friends,

Words fail to express my deepest sympathy for you. As St. Paul says, "Sorrow not as the world sorrows," but that does not make the pain, the loneliness, and the empty arms any less. I take comfort in the words of a our Savior, "I am the resurrection and the life, he that believeth in me though he die, shall live." This verse has been such comfort that I had it carved on our little daughter Gladys' flower bed. Your sorrow is greater than mine. I had the satisfaction of nursing Gladys for three months. I was sort of prepared for what I had to go through. But you are so far away and no doubt you least expected to hear such shocking news.

George Herbert was good enough when he heard the news to call William [her son] and tell him the sad news. I thought of you both and pray for you whenever I am awake—a little prayer is ascended to our heavenly Father who alone is able to comfort his children.

I will close with my deepest sympathy. I am as ever you friend and co-worker in the Master's Vineyard,

(signed) Matilda K. Paul Tamaree

They had given up their little girl when they sent her to school in the East. Now they had given up to eternity the young woman who had blossomed with motherhood. Mercifully their deeply ingrained acceptance of God's will, strengthened through years of practice, would have tempered their terrible pain.

KETCHIKAN

When Mr. and Mrs. George J. Beck arrived in Ketchikan in the fall of 1930, they were not strangers to the city since they had often been there on the Lois to hold mission services. The people in Ketchikan were delighted to have them, but the flock left in Hoonah were bereft. A letter from Frank St. Clair expresses the sadness they felt at his leaving.

Dear friend,
I will write just a few lines to you this evening to let you know about ourselves. We are all well here but some times we feel lonesome. It is very hard to forget you. Every day they talk about you, some of our people.
We expect to see you here. I don't understand why. We all know you went out from here for good but we feel just like our father is dead. We are all disappointed every day and I don't believe we can find a man like you and so wish you will not forget us in your prayers.

He discussed facts and figures about the foundation he was digging for the dam and hydroelectric pla t being built in Hoonah and asked for advice on problems he had encountered. Then he returned to their memories of him.

As soon as we go up the Dam we always remember you just because you did a good job for us. Every day we always talk about you. Sometimes they see your spirit up the Dam therefore I believe your body went down to Ketchikan. Your spirit is up at the dam yet.

Construction of a new church building in Ketchikan was the first item on the agenda. The town church had grown out of a mission begun by Edward Marsden, a former Sitka Industrial School student who had been commissioned as a Presbyterian minister to Saxman in 1898. As the population in Saxman dwindled, Reverend Marsden began to work more in Ketchikan where the population was growing. In March of 1925, forty-one people signed a petition to organize a church in Ketchikan and presented it at the spring meeting of the Presbytery, which acted on the petition fa-

Ketchikan

Mr. and Mrs Beck in Ketchikan, 1930.

vorably and appointed a committee to consummate the organization by June. Among the signers were William Kinninook and Joe Johnson, grandfather and uncle respectively of present day resident Mary Baines Jones, who was able to furnish the original list. Other present day families represented were the Murchisons, Verneys, Haldanes, Dundases, Peels, Burtons, Inmans, Fawcettes, Leasks, Calvins, Eatons, Bryants, Lawsons, Booths, McKays, Daltons, and Millers.

During 1925 the Ketchikan mission became a full fledged church under the leadership of Reverend Fred Falconer, in a one-story peak-roofed building at 123 Stedman Street, where radio station KRBD stands today. Since the original structure was considered not worth the expense of repairing, Reverend Falconer began a campaign in 1927 for a new building.

This was the situation Reverend Beck inherited with his new post, and several letters on the particulars of the new building were exchanged with the Home Board of Missions. In a letter dated December 27,1931, Dr. A.J. Montgomery from the Board of Missions at first expressed disappointment at being unable to place Reverend Falconer in another mission and then went on to discuss matters of the building. The board had agreed to a previous request by Reverend Falconer to give $5,000 to be matched by local funds for a church to cost no more than $10,000. Mr. Montgomery said that Dr. Matthew had asked for $10,000 for a white church in Ketchikan but had been refused since the Board was committed to helping missions for the natives. In the same letter he mentioned that he had a senior in

Ketchikan

seminary with experience in farm work pledged to go to Hoonah the following May. The young man had been recommended as having unusual ability and a desire to donate his life to work in Alaska just as those working in the foreign field. " I am hoping he will be able to pick up the threads of your work and go ahead with it."

In a January 1931 letter, Mr. Montgomery said he would do his best to promote Mr. Beck's plans for a church building, as Ketchikan was next in line for a building project. But the effects of 1929 depression had forced the Board to cut the budget for the year.

> *"It is very difficult to convey to people who live in Alaska the seriousness of the financial situation here. We have bread lines in all the big cities. Last Saturday there was a food riot in one of the Southern States. Most people can not remember when times were harder than they are now. This necessarily reflects itself in the giving of the churches to the boards. . . .Barring emergencies that can not be foreseen, the Ketchikan enterprise should come next in Alaska and the Board will get to this just as soon as its income will justify it."*

Ketchikan Presbyterian Church in 1930.   Ketchikan Museums 80.2.7.1.

Ketchikan

A third letter from Mr. Montgomery in March mentioned that he would be giving Mr. Beck's plans to their architect to estimate a cost and would present them to the building committee in April. He especially appreciated the detailed information "by means of ground plans and elevation," which were probably better laid out than most because of Reverend Beck's training and experience with buildings and their foundations. Then an April 29 letter announced that the Board had awarded $3640 from the budget and $3900 from the grants fund toward the new Ketchikan church. Mr. Montgomery instructed Mr. Beck to see whether a contractor thought the building could be erected for that amount.—$7540. By July 13, 1931, the Board Treasurer had authorized Gene C. Gould as the agent to disburse the funds—a go-ahead signal for building the church. Several communications discussed the progress of the building. By December the building was up, and Sunday attendance had increased to 175 people. Since there was $788.46 left in the fund, Mr. Beck asked whether some of it might be spent on new pews, as he felt the old benches spoiled the appearance of the church. In January 1932 Mr. Montgomery expressed the board's great delight at the overage and heartily approved the expenditure of up to $500 for pews. "If you could . . . then send back to the Board a check of $288.46, it would do a great deal to hearten the board.

In his letter Mr. Montgomery had also congratulated Ketchikan on its splendid plant and expressed his own satisfaction that in that year, the hardest in its history, the Home Missions had been able to build new plants in Fairbanks, Wrangell and Ketchikan. Mr. Beck reported to Mr. Montgomery that $489.50 had been returned, explaining, "We could only do this by giving up many things we need in the new building and untold hours of labor on our part." They had built twenty-nine pews "of the finest fir" after having examined pews in all the other churches. Sunday evening for a Washington's birthday celebration they had over 200 in attendance. He especially thanked Mr. Montgomery for his efforts in appropriating the money. "We know if it had not been for your active interest in our work it could never have been done."

A journal beginning in December of 1931 gives some idea of the daily routine of the Becks. But since the journal recorded church activity, it did not mention that their son George had started Service Electric Company with Bill Wikstrom in 1931 or that on March 29 of that year he and his wife

Ketchikan

George J. Beck in the Pulpit.

Marjorie had had a daughter whom they named Suzanne.

According to the journal, the new church was up but unfinished, yet the Reverend Beck conducted services there anyway. It still needed pews and a hot water supply to the kitchen and several finishing touches, which he and several employed members were working on. The worship hall stood at the left as one entered the building. Its stained glass windows had been ordered to fit the woodwork frames made by the pastor, who was himself a master woodworker. The social hall was to the right and behind it a kitchen. Upstairs were the Becks' apartment, across the front of the building, and to the rear, a smaller apartment and a storeroom.

The journal noted that on December 12 John Rose was buried. On December 13 deacons, elders, and deaconesses were ordained for the Saxman and Ketchikan congregations. Ketchikan church deacons ordained were Mrs. Jacob Thomas and Heber Reese; elders, Simon Dalton and Jacob Thomas; and deaconess, Mrs. Maud Atkinson. Those ordained from Saxman were elders, John Jackson and Mark Williams; deacons, Frank Howard and James Klindow; and deaconesses, Mrs. Peter McKay and Mrs. Charles Johnson. The Ketchikan choir, which was organized December 11, sang its first piece with Miss Morgan playing the organ.

The journal entries are brief jottings, generally of ordinary happenings with a tragic events appearing suddenly among them, more poignant for being so unexpected. On December 14 Reverend Beck buried infant Thomas Valensuelo and attended the funeral of Helen Dempsey. He also started putting a hot water tank in the church kitchen, which he finished within the next two days. The next morning he called at the mink ranch of Alec

Ketchikan

Cameron to talk over the funeral of Jack Daley, who had killed himself after shooting to death Helen Dempsey. He held the funeral service for Jack Daly that afternoon. William Paul visited that evening. Entries continue in this vein.

December 16: Eighteen out for prayer meeting. Joe Johnson took charge of testimony meeting. In business meeting afterwards arrangements were made for Christmas tree program on December 23. Joe Johnson in charge of decorations. Christmas tree lights were bought from Service Electric. Alec Cameron gave us some halibut today [possibly in appreciation for giving the funeral service for Jack Daley].

December 17: Paid Kehoe for bond for contractor [who built church]. The children practiced their pieces for the Christmas program, twenty-two numbers in all. Attended Pioneer meeting and afterwards attended a reception for William Paul given by the ANB. The Sisterhood was present and served coffee and sandwiches to the 60 people present, including members from Saxman.

December 18: Visited Marge and Susie. Joe Johnson brought in tree and greens for decoration. Choir practice with Miss Morgan playing. Saturday took passage on USCG Alert for Metlakatla at 11:30 am. Rough trip, but had a good time there. Returned on the Eskimo and got to bed at 2 .am.

December 22: Spent day decorating tree and hall and choir practice. Letter from the Board authorized the church to spend part of the balance from the building fund for lumber for pews. In the evening I went across the street to a Salvation Army coffee and sale.

December 23: Over 400 people attended the Christmas exercises this evening, a very successful affair. None of the children forgot their parts and the choir sang beautifully.

December 24: Cleaned church and returned Salvation Army seats. Walked to Saxman and took part in Christmas exercises, which came off well. Walked home.

December 25, Christmas: Spent the day with Marge and George and family. Great Dinner. Dr. Rhone and his wife were there too.

December 26: Drew up plans for pews.

December 27: No services in church since all attended opening of new Salvation Army hall. One hundred fifty present. J. R. Heckman and Mr. Armor were in charge. Walked to Saxman for service. Florist gave me a

Ketchikan

lift. Walked back to Christian Endeavor and evening service.

During the next week he started Sully on the pews first thing, talked to Talbott about prospecting, had his picture taken for Pioneer and American Legion halls, and called on the Lutheran minister to look over pews in his church.

December 30: Attended Chamber of Commerce noon meeting at the Blue Fox and heard a talk on the herring situation. Ends of church pews with the seats were delivered this afternoon. Attended the funeral service for Mr. Hiri who was burned to death last Sunday. Buddy was down this afternoon but did not stay. Mr. Fisher framed sailor picture for the Legion this evening and is working on two others.

December 31: Made several calls on Saxman people today: George McKay baby, Howard; John Jackson and family; Mrs. Parick, teacher. Was given a lift in three different cars. Several people who had borrowed differing amounts of money repaid it. [Church evidently lent money to members in need.] Attended Pioneer meeting and was elected historian. Held a Watch meeting, after which Mr. and Mrs. Cameron and Mr. Pettybone called and had coffee and cake [which Mrs. Beck probably prepared and served].

January 1, New Year's: Rested a bit and visited Marge and George. Visited people in the hospital.

January 2, 1932: Took my best suit to cleaners this morning and it is to be returned at 4 p.m. Turned in Picture of U.S.S. Mongolia to get reprinted by Mr. Fisher, who will also frame the picture of Mt. Edgecumbe.

January 3, Sunday: Held church services and went to Saxman, where Casper Mather spoke. Mrs. Beck went to hear the singers from the Christian church in Metlakatla who were singing at the Redmen's hall. The sixty members were invited to supper in the Presbyterian social hall and entertained by the Women's Missionary society. Got to bed at 2:30 a.m.

January 4: Did not sleep in the next morning but set to work at 6:30 a.m. on pews, aided by Jacob Thomas, George Eaton, and Heber Reese. Simon Dalton painted the church floor. Walked to Saxman and held session meeting. Walked half way back, then picked up by Bob Killewatch. Had trouble with oil burner in church and then slipped on newly painted church floor and ruined my newly cleaned suit. Attended American Legion meeting, where the Mongolia picture was duly received and

Ketchikan

hung on the wall.

January 5: Joe Johnson joined Eaton and Thomas in working the whole day with me in assembling the pews. Simon Dalton and Heber Reese put a second coat of paint on the church floor. All worked again on Wednesday.

January 6: Finished the last bench. I was installed as historian of Pioneers and attended Christian Endeavor meeting. Spent some time with Reverend Falconer, the pastor who preceded me, who is visiting in town and staying with Mr. Foss.

January 8: Held choir practice and afterwards played piano with Joel Baines on the trombone and Joe Johnson on the coronet until eleven. Mr. Reese was paid for painting. Continued working on installing seats. Mr. Dalton was paid for church work. A parishioner promised to pay money borrowed last year.

January 12: Seats all installed. Talked with government doctor but he saw no hope for a native hospital in Ketchikan.

January 15: Ordered lumber and worked on building crib for Marge [Susie would have been nine months old]. The Metlakatla band gave a benefit performance for Red Cross and was entertained at lunch by the Presbyterian Ladies' Society. Others guests included Reverend Walker, Mr. and Mrs. J. R. Heckman, Mrs. Ross, Mr. Larson, and Mr. and Mrs. Sandburn and daughter. Have been on call for jury duty for a week but have not been called.

January 18: Worked most of day finishing Kiddy Koop for Susie. Did not paint it. Visit from George and family.

January 19: Stained and varnished a table for the church. Sent off pension dues.

January 20: Church dinner at Saxman. Christian Endeavor meeting, with Mr. and Mrs. Ed Ridley of Episcopalian church and Mr. Majury of Salvation Army present. I played the organ. Came home to Women's group meeting waiting for me to decide on dinner to be given for Metlakatla choir on Sunday.

January 22, Friday: Turned out at 6 a.m., remodeled blackboard, and put out notice of concert Sunday. Wrote invitation to Reverend Marsden [to dinner after choir performance]. Put newly finished table in church. Mr. Cameron at Cold Storage will give 12 pounds of salmon for the dinner

Ketchikan

Sunday. After choir practice Mr. and Mrs. Baines served lunch.

January 24: Good morning service but no evening service because of the sacred concert at the Lutheran Church. Entertained seventy at dinner for Metlakatla choir members at l0:30 p.m. Bed at 2 a.m.

The next few days were extremely cold and water pipes froze and broke at Episcopal church building. Service Electric and son George had had twelve pipe-thawing jobs in one day. In early February he talked with Reverend Walker about Red Cross aid for Simon Dalton. He called to see Dr. Rhone about John Jackson but did not get to see the doctor as there were too many before him. Two days later he filled out forms for John Jackson to be admitted into Marine hospital. Extreme cold persisted and a gas boat exploded in harbor, too far out for the fire engine to reach. The boat was totaled. He had reported all week to court but was not called to serve until February 4 when he was retained on the Hyda Boose case where Attorney Ziegler was lawyer for defense. Two days later a verdict was rendered: not guilty for inadequate warrant. The same day he received letters from Emery Tobin asking that they be signed and sent to Washington protesting against the repeal of the Alaska Bone Dry law. He practiced on the organ playing the hymns to be sung Sunday.

February 6: Held meeting in church to comfort parents of baby Frances Bryant. Had funeral service next day. Buddy stayed with us both nights as Marge has had very bad cold.

February 8: Attended American Legion meeting and acted as chaplain. Was also called upon for a speech.

February 9: Called on Jack Talbott, who had been ill, the George Inman family, and Mrs. Atkinson. Stopped along the way to talk with a lot of children. Called at Mr. Charles' place to discuss Pioneers' Washington Birthday program. Walked to and from Saxman. Lent money to several parishioners [It is not clear whether it is his own money or from a church fund. Some but not all pay it back.]

February 12: The 18-month-old daughter Josephine of Mr. and Mrs. Alec Bryant died this morning. The Bryants were also the parents of Baby Thomas who died earlier in the month. Mr. Dunn agreed to speak at the Washington Birthday program on February 25. Called at the Bryant house and afterwards called on Mrs. Baines. Later tried to have meeting with Mrs. Alec Bryant to make funeral arrangements, but she was too ill to talk

Ketchikan

with us. On the way home we came upon a very drunk man, whom Joe Johnson and I took home.

February 13: Funeral for Josephine Bryant. Mr. Dyer played and Mrs. George Luman and Mrs. Annie Leask sang a duet. Twenty were in attendance. George took us to Saxman for services and took Mrs. Beck back with him. I stayed longer and came back with Pat Hollywood. Buddy stayed with us Friday and Saturday nights.

February 16: Reverend Swanson arrived on the Princeton. I spent some time with him and he had dinner with us. Reverend Swanson held the Prayer meeting the next night and visited with us until midnight.

February 19: Reverend Sam Davis appointed postmaster at Hydaburg. Son George lowest bidder on the wiring of the new building being erected at the sawmill.

February 20: Buried poor Manley today. Killed himself with drink. Found dead in bed with his shoes and overcoat on. No friends, not even enough to carry the coffin. I read the commitment service and led prayers at the grave.

February 22: Attended the Washington celebration at the Redmen's hall—375 present.

February 23: Attended service at Graham's Undertaking for the 23-year-old son of Reverend Mather.

February 25: Attended funeral of Reverend Mather's son Victor. The worst storm of the season. Rain and wind in torrents. A large crowd walked through it all to the grave. John Dunn gave fine talk at Pioneer Washington Day celebration.

February 27: Stopped at hospital to see how John Jackson was getting on. Found him in fine shape. Operated upon yesterday. No pain at all this morning.

February 28: George and Marge spent next evening with us.

March 1: Was paid $90 by the court today and deposited it in bank. Took Mr. Troast and George out to dinner, then took Troast down to Ridleys and made plans for a special meeting to talk about the Shoemaker School tomorrow evening. Heard over the radio that the Lindberg Baby had been stolen. The next day Mr. Troast spoke to the Chamber of Commerce about the Shoemaker Boys school. One hundred in attendance.

The journal did not mention the items discussed in correspondence be-

Ketchikan

tween Mr. Beck and the Board. By early March all the finances of the new church were settled and there were letters discussing the dedication that was set for April. Mr. Beck replied with disappointment to Reverend Saunders' statement that he might not be able to attend the dedication. He felt that a "presence" from the Board would greatly enhance the joyful feelings of the church members at the dedication celebration. In the same letter he noted that Ketchikan had been, inadvertently he hoped, excluded from the budget, and he objected to the fact that two newer ministers were being paid at a higher rate than the older ones. "They may be good men, but they would have to work twenty-five hours a day to do more than some of the rest of us are trying to do."

March 9: Choir practice for an hour to get ready for music festival. Received final jury duty check for $15, making total $105. Some parishioners repaid loans and others borrowed. Bought a new black hat. Mr. and Mrs. Twon of Sheldon Jackson School visited on way to Tokeen Marble Works.

March 11: Married Harold C. Jones and Evelyn Rowan at 6:30 p.m. Finished printing report of expenditures on the church building: Total spent: $9,483.36. Total received from all sources: $9,972.86. Returned to Home Missions Board: $489.50. Gave copies of report to Tongass Trading, the bank, Mr. Steppe, and Service Electric. Visited nine patients in the hospital. March 14 received letter from the Board thanking me for returning $489.50 from building fund. Letters from Reverend Saunders saying they cannot attend dedication of church. Visited Joe Johnson, who has been quite ill.

March 15: Had funeral service for Carl Johnson. My cold is quite bad. I was sick for three days and did little work but did attend Chamber of Commerce and Pioneer meetings.

March 19: Sent the Paul family their church letters. Attended Salvation Army sing, but it was mostly Presbyterians. Buddy is here.

March 21: Much better today, although cold is hanging on. Mr. Parrott tuned both pianos. Paid the eight dollar charge from my own funds. ANB meeting at the church.

March 24: Visited sick people on north end of town and mailed invitations to an upcoming social. Attended Pioneers and read a letter in memory of Carl Johnson.

March 27, Easter Sunday: 40 present at church; 30 at Sunday school ;

Ketchikan

35 at Saxman; 25 at Christian Endeavor at 3 p.m. George's little girl Susie baptized, 65 present.

March 28: Held funeral for infant son of John Jackson; the reverends Mather and Majury were present. For next two days worked in church and practiced with choir. Gave short address at Seaman's center at a farewell luncheon for Brother Atkins—150 present.

March 31: My 61st birthday. Lunch at Pioneers and another lunch given by Christian Endeavor, a surprise for my birthday. They gave me a very nice card and a necktie. Dinner at Marge and George's.

April 1: Loaned money to several parishioners. Good choir practice; choir in good shape for dedication. Miss Clem and the other teachers gathered the children together in the Presbyterian hall to hear Reverend Mather and William Paul speak. Visited eight sick families.

April 5, Tuesday: The Presbyterian church was dedicated tonight at the evening service. Most of the Presbyterian ministers of the churches of Southeast Alaska and all of the Ketchikan Protestant churches were present.

The journal ended at this date with the dedication of the church.

In July 1932 upon learning of Dr. A. J. Montgomery's approaching retirement, Reverend Beck wrote him that he and the entire presbytery of Alaska felt a deep sense of loss in his leaving the Board. "We know you have had our interests at heart and it will be a long time before any one else can take the place you have made in our hearts." He continued further along, "I am so sorry Mr. Saunders is going to leave the work. What is the matter with our young ministers? Many who are willing to make the sacrifice demanded by this work up here don't seem to have the ability to do the work, and those who have the ability don't seem to have the spirit of sacrifice. There are times when I almost get discouraged."

The February 1933 Verstovian announced that three ministers had visited Sheldon Jackson school for the February 4 weekend: Reverend and Mrs. Waggoner, Reverend Beck of Ketchikan, and Reverend Pederson of Wrangell. Reverend Beck presided at morning services; Reverend Waggoner spoke in Sunday school, and Reverend Pederson spoke at evening service at the chapel down town. In April 1933 the paper reported that Rev. George J. Beck was elected moderator of the Presbytery in Southeast Alaska.

August 1934 brought what was probably the most devastating event to occur in his life. Harriet, his wife of thirty-four years, died after a short

Ketchikan

illness. An announcement in the Ketchikan Daily News stated that Mrs. George H. Beck and her two children were returning from Seattle on the Aleutian and would be there for the funeral services. Bud, who was nine at the time, does not remember the service, but he remembers rushing back to Ketchikan for it. Frank Parrish, a friend with Westinghouse with whom they had been staying, had just put them on a train to visit Marge's Aunt Jess in South Bend, Washington. Returning to Westinghouse, just a short distance away, he found the telegram announcing Mrs. Beck's death and rushed back to the train station on time to tell them the news and get them off the train. He took them instead to Alaska Steamship Company and made arrangements for them to take the S.S. Aleutian to Ketchikan.

The Daily News article reported further that the reverends Russell Pederson of Wrangell and A.D. Swogger of Metlakatla would conduct the funeral services as well as the usual Sunday morning and evening services of the congregation for the week. "Mrs. Beck died in her home Wednesday morning, succumbing to a heart ailment that had been affecting her for several years and from which she suffered a severe attack Tuesday night. Her burial will be in the Pioneer plot in the Ketchikan cemetery."

Whenever asked how he was able to accomplish so much often in times of great adversity, his answer was, "My wife was of inestimable help." Genevieve Mayberry paraphrased him in her biography, "Mrs. Beck was a true helpmate in their years together. With deep insight and boundless ability, she was teacher, doctor, nurse, and sympathetic mentor to all who needed counsel."

Harriet Weaver Beck is rarely mentioned in the available letters, which were generally business related, or the diaries, which were mainly for keeping a record of church activities and expenses to be reported monthly to the Home Mission Board. But a letter from Mr. Beck to his relatives in New York on September 10, 1934, told of her last moments and revealed so much about this faithful and uncomplaining helpmate about whom so little is known.

My dear People,
    The only excuse I can offer for not writing you before this is that my eyes and heart have gone back on me every time I have tried to put down on paper the things we want you to know.

Ketchikan

We did not realize it, but Harriet had been failing for some time past and the wonder of it all is that she remained with us as long as she did. There were no last messages as none of us ever thought the time had come. A great change had been taking place during the past two years. She was growing sweeter all the time, always talking lovingly about all of you, time after time sitting down to write but for some reason she could not and her letters have been few and far between.

As I look back over the years we spent together, I feel so unworthy of the privilege that was mine of serving with her. The world will never how hard she worked in the building of the Master's Kingdom in this rugged old world.

She loved pretty, dainty things and her body was never very strong, but because she felt the call of God to carry His message to the rough places of the world she put her hand to the plow and would not look back. She gave up so much that others might have the beautiful things of life.

She gave to the world a son and daughter who were the highlights of her life and who just filled her life with joy. After Kosseyia was called home, Margie meant so much to her and her four little grandchildren remain to bless the world.

There is so much I would like to tell you but I cannot.

It was such a joy that these last years could be spent with the children here in Ketchikan. George through his electric shop and generous terms enabled us to install many appliances that were a great comfort to her. She just had to push a button and much of her work was done. She hardly ever missed a church service, but of late the trip downstairs was quite a journey. All the planes every day flew by her windows, twelve navy planes were in sight at one time anchored on each side of the channel. The great ships sailed by and the little fishing boats (hundreds of them) sailed into the harbor right under her living room windows. Our moonlight nights are so wonderful and at the entrance to our harbor there are two lights, one red and one green, that flash at intervals all night. When the time is right the moon shines right between them, a great broad band of silver showing the salmon passing up the river amid showers of sparkling spray and just across the channel the dark green of the cedars

Ketchikan

with the mountains.

Her last days with us were especially happy. The only cloud was that Margie and the children were away for awhile in Seattle. Little Suzanne and her grandmother loved each other so. George was staying with us. Many of the ships of the Navy visited us this summer. I held a special service on the flagship and they called for us with a most beautiful launch from the ship. Harriet was well enough to go on that trip. The District Governor of the International Rotary Club made a trip to Ketchikan. Harriet was an honored guest at a banquet given him at the Legion cabin. It was one of those beautiful evenings enjoyed only in this part of the world. There have been several notable services at the church. She has welcomed many teachers and missionaries as they passed through. Thousands of tourists have stopped here. Ketchikan is noted for its rainfall, but this summer has given us more sunshine than we have ever known before.

Sunday morning she attended service and then rested for the remainder of the day. Monday she did not feel so well, having trouble with what was thought to be indigestion. She had had so many spells of this nature that she would not let me call a doctor. She was not well enough to see callers that afternoon. Harriet loved to ride, and George wanted to take her out, but she did not feel able. Tuesday morning found her a bit better but she did not get up till late in the afternoon. She wanted to cook the dinner, but she sat in the big chair while I did it. The three of us—Mother, George and I—enjoyed the meal together. It was a very happy hour, the last one we shall ever spend in that way.

After dinner George bundled her up and took her out to the end of the new road just opened. It was a thirty mile ride; he did not drive fast and the ride was comfortable. Much of the way lay along the seashore. The sun playing on the calm sea, showing through the cedars, ferns, and flowers, and the bushes bending with great clusters of ripe berries made such a wonderful picture that she exclaimed many times over the beauty of it all.

I had a very important meeting in town that evening and did not get home until ten-thirty. George had to put the car away. She felt so good after the ride, and because there was no one to stop her she began to do some housework. However when I got home she was in

Ketchikan

bed feeling ill. At midnight she let me call the doctor. He saw at once it was her heart but never for one moment thought the end was near. He remained with us for two hours and told me what to do and promised to be back at eight the next morning. I thought it was but another weak spell, for her arms often became numb and I would rub them. Her last words expressed her thoughtfulness for me, for she said, "Don't rub anymore, dear, you will tire yourself out."

At four o'clock I thought she was going to sleep as the doctor had said she would. I went into the next room, returning in a few moments and her breathing did not seem natural. When I spoke to her she did not answer. I then took her hand and for the first time in all these long beautiful years together there was no response. Then a few long deep breaths and her great loving heart ceased to beat. She entered into rest at thirty minutes past four, Wednesday morning, August 15, 1934. George was with me and we took the blow together. He was and is a great tower of strength and comfort to me.

It was a great comfort to us both the way our little city rallied to help. The U.S. Military cable office contacted Margie at Seattle and in half an hour had an answer back. The Alaska Steamship company, even though all reservations were sold out for weeks ahead, managed in some way to get Margie and the children on board a fast steamer within a few hours. Reverend Pederson came down from Wrangell and took charge. George was wonderful. I felt so guilty leaving so much to him when his heart was so burdened. Reverend Swogger came over from Metlakatla. The different churches, the Native people, the American Legion, the fire department, in fact the whole city seemed to take it as a personal matter. And oh! the flowers. I did not know such wonderful ones could be produced in Alaska. Yours, Father, Alfred, and Lulu contained such beautiful roses and other flowers.

The services at the church were beautiful and as the procession formed, the police stopped all traffic. It had been cloudy all day but just as the last words were said at the cemetery, the sun came out so warm with such fullness of glory that the commander of the Legion, whose men were pall bearers, said to me, "What a wonderful benediction at the close of a beautiful life." Two hours later I went back to the cemetery. It is a beautiful spot on quite an elevation overlook-

ing an arm of the sea she loved so well. The city is spending quite a bit of money there. A caretaker is always in attendance. The trees, flowers, and grass are kept trimmed and as I looked at the place where her dear body rested, I saw the mound itself and the lot on either side covered eighteen inches deep with the most beautiful flowers that grow. The florist was sold out. He could not fill many of the orders our friends sent in.

In Alaska she had spent most of her life in glorious service and here I am sure she wanted her body to rest surrounded by the great mountains she so dearly loved. I am sending you a picture of Mt. Edgecumbe, her pet of them all. It is an old volcano nearly four thousand feet high. Twice she climbed to the very top and slept in the crater.

As soon as he could speak after Harriet's death, George said, "We must get Marge back here. She will help us." So she came and has done so much to help lift the burden. Little Suzanne does not quite understand it all, but she throws her arms about my neck and says, "I will take care of you, Grandpa." Buddy sleeps often with me at the manse and is a great comfort. One night he was lying on his little cot at the foot of my bed and he said, "Grandpa, it doesn't make any difference how happy we are on earth, we can't be as happy as Grandma is in heaven."

I am sure this is but part of the Master's great plan and is as it should be, but she has become so great a part of my life it seems as though the earth has fallen away from under me. I do not know what the plan before me is. I am just waiting. He will make it clear.

With much love to all of you from George, Margie, Buddy, and Suzanne, I am Lovingly yours, (signed) George

The Pioneer Auxiliary gave Mrs. Beck the following tribute: "She was a pioneer of Alaska by her own right and a member of Pioneer Auxiliary No. 7, a woman loved and respected by all who knew her. Her sweet disposition and lovable nature drew to her many friends. She was a woman of humble character, who through years of devotion to her family and helpfulness in the mission field, endeared herself to all. We know there is no death where the memory of a beautiful, wholesome and helpful life lives on."

Ketchikan

There would have been letters and condolences from relatives and friends throughout Alaska, but none have survived. Records and letters exist for certain periods in the Becks' lives but are missing entirely for other periods, which suggest that boxes of them were probably destroyed in some way. The October 1934 Verstovian said in reporting her death, "Mrs. Beck came to teach in the Sitka Training school January 28, 1893, as Harriet Weaver. Two years later Mr. Beck also came as a teacher. They were married the following year. Mrs. Beck taught here for twenty years and after that served as a pastor's wife at Hoonah and Ketchikan."

Reverend Beck continued to live in the manse holding services, performing weddings and funerals, visiting the sick, and pursuing other pastoral duties. In January of 1936 a letter from Anthony Dimond, Alaska delegate, states that he had written in Mr. Beck's behalf that he be considered honorably discharged from the the military service of the United States for his work on the US Transport Mongolia during World War I. Then a letter from Mr. Dimond dated March 23 stated that the bill was denied.

> *I regret to have to say that the sub-committee [of the House Committee on Military Affairs] informed me that there was no possibility that the bill could be favorably reported and passed. It was said that there are some thousands of others in the same status and that it would not be advisable to pass a bill granting the equivalent of an honorable discharge to one and not take care of the others. It may be that eventually Congress will undertake some such general legislation.*

In 1936 at the age of sixty-five, Reverend Beck retired officially from the ministry, but he continued to substitute as minister whenever needed. At one time he served as pastor for a year at the Ketchikan church before a replacement could be found. Letters show that his pension amounted to $50 a month, which the Board enhanced by another $27.36, which should have started in April of 1936. Like so many bureaucracies, that of the Board was rusty at times and by December he had still not received any of the $27.36 checks. To the administrators in New York, the missionaries in the fields were often just names and numbers. When he visited the main office in the April 1936, nobody mentioned his work or asked about the ministry in Alaska, nor were they able to find a church for him to deliver his Alaska message. He felt like discarded goods and wrote to Reverend Arthur Limouze, Secretary of the Board, "as a friend, not as a member of the Board," since Rev. Limouze and his wife had spent some time at the Ketchikan station and had become friends of the Becks.

> *Last spring as you know after nine years of daily service without a vacation, and a full forty years service in the field I made the trip back to New York at my own expense, with the exception of $28 fare to Seattle. Calling at the Board rooms, I was kindly received by a few of the officers. Aside from this, I was not asked a question about the work; my years of service were not recognized in any way. After visiting with my folks for a few weeks, I offered my services as a missionary speaker, for I have a message. Mr. Somerndike wrote me it was impossible to find a church that would hear me and that he could get me a pass back to Seattle as soon as I wished to go. I could only feel that in the eyes of the Board my work of a lifetime had been a failure."*

Reverend Limouze answered apologizing for the difficulty and explaining that promotion of missionary work was done in the fall and winter, "when there would have been all sorts of calls for the sort of thing I know you can do so well." Both men had lost their wives in recent years. "I think we both understand something of the loss that each is sustaining and can appreciate just what this Christmas means without the one that has been so large in our lives. . . . Personally, I want you to know how warm a place you have in my heart. There are some friendships that mean a great deal in life and yours is one of them. Somehow you have seemed near to me because Mrs. Beck and Mrs. Limouze were so fond of each other."

The following week a letter arrived from Reverend Somerndike apologizing for the oversight on his $27.36 check, which was in addition to the regular pension fund of $50 given "as an expression of the Board's affection for one who has served in the mission field in a spirit of unusual self-sacrifice."

On his retirement Mr. Beck left the apartment that had served as the manse and moved in with his son and daughter-in-law and their children, where he would stay until he was hospitalized in 1960. His grandchildren meant much to him. On moving into his children's home Mr. Beck had immediately set to work building a shop in the back yard with an upstairs to be a playhouse for five-year-old Susie. That way he had both grandchildren close to him. Eleven-year-old Bud especially enjoyed spending time with his grandfather. Bud worked alongside his grandfather and got his basic training in carpentry, at which he still excels. He still uses power tools his grandfather bought for them to use in their work. Bud's friend Ralph Bartholomew, who lived a few houses away and was at Becks' often, mentioned much later in life that he had learned his carpentry skills from Mr. Beck. Bud and his grandfather built a small rowboat which Bud remembers rowing many an afternoon between Ketchikan and Pennock Island. There was a nice sandy beach at the top of the island on the westward side where the swimming was good. He also remembers going there with friends later as teenagers in a larger boat his grandfather had had built and equipped with a one and on-half horsepower engine.

Another death occurred in 1939, that of Mr. Beck's father at 94 in 1939 in New York. The elder George Beck's obituary referred to him as a sculptor whose works are displayed in world-famed museums. "Statues grace the austere halls of the Metropolitan Museum of Art in New York City, the Museum of Arts and Sciences and The Brooklyn Institute of Arts and Crafts. Mr. Beck was also a numismatist of international repute and the medals he created won awards at several fairs, including exhibitions in Paris, Sydney, Chicago and the Philadelphia sesquicentennial."

RETIREMENT

When the United States entered into World War II in 1941, Alaskans were even more affected than most Americans, especially after the Japanese landed on Attu in the Aleutian Islands. Even in tiny Ketchikan, on a small island thousands of miles southeast of Attu, families began to move south and young men volunteered for the military. At the age of seventy Mr. Beck felt he still had something to offer and volunteered as a chaplain to the service men at the military airport near Metlakatla, a small town on Annette Island, the only person serving that post for two years.

Since travel between the Army Airforce base and Ketchikan was too time consuming Mr. Beck stayed at the base most of the time. Bud remembers visiting him there as a teenager and making some of the rounds with him. One time they rode from the military post to Point Davidson where there was a coast artillery placement, which consisted of a large gun mounted on a rotating base, turning on circular track embedded in concrete and manned by military personnel. After they visited with the men there, they crossed on a sandbar to a tide island in the bay where three more men manned the lookout station. The servicemen were not much older than eighteen and were really happy to have visitors. Bud remembers noticing how isolated they were and how lonely a job it was.

With an understanding of their difficulties and an indomitable sense of fun and good humor, Mr. Beck won the love and devotion and respect of the men. But he also won the highest admiration of their commanders, as is shown from letters in the files of the Board National Missions. Lieutenant Colonel Ellis G. Christian states, "It is my belief that more than one other single factor, your work here is responsible for the excellent morale of the troops here." Chief of Chaplains, William R. Arnold, says, "The loyalty, patriotism, and devotion which you are manifesting by your unselfish labors are an inspiration to all of us. The many individuals whom you served during the last war, as well as those whom you are now serving, owe you an enormous debt of gratitude." Even Harold "Hap" Arnold, General of the Army, wrote his appreciation:"We hope you feel the warm affection and profound, lasting gratitude of each individual officer and enlisted man whom you helped. . .How you found the time to do so much for so many we do not know, but we do know that not one of those men

Retirement

will ever forget the comfort you gave him at a time when those priceless things were so desperately needed....It is just such intangibles as these that contributed notably to the success of our most difficult and important missions."

In 1942 in gratitude for his work as chaplain to the military forces at the base on Annette Island during World War II, Captain R. O. Zimmerling painted Reverend Beck's portrait. Then Heinrich Bruener of Ketchikan carved a frame in the form of an endless chain with small anchors in each corner in recognition of Reverend Beck's service as chaplain with the United States Navy during World War I. The framed portrait was presented to him at the Annette base that same year by Lt. Colonel Ellis Christensen. In the early 1990's the portrait was presented by the family to Sheldon Jackson College.

Kosseyia's son Wayne Duff mentioned from letters his grandfather had written to the family that the top military officer in Alaska, Simon Bolivar Buckner, became a good friend of Mr. Beck and took him on some of the General's visits to the interior. These were working trips and Reverend Beck ministered to the troops. Wayne has one note written on the back of a photograph that reads, "This is how I look riding in a jeep over the mountains before daylight in the morning when it is below zero. Uncle Sam takes good care of his own. I do not hate the Japanese or the Germans but am ready to fight them to a finish. I would be glad to help them get back on their feet again after we have taken their ships, planes, and guns."

After the war Mr. Beck continued to live with his family. He walked to town daily, visiting with people along the way or at lunch at the Blue Fox or resting in the lobby of the Ingersoll Hotel. Bud graduated from high school in 1944 but was kept out of the service by a deaf ear from an infection he had contracted in the summer of 1940. After having the ear lanced twice failed to solve the problem, Bud underwent a mastoidectomy. Then he developed meningitis, which was life-threatening for a while, and Marge, who was in Seattle, was wired to return home. In a letter notifying Marge of the surgery, George said of his father, "I am sure thankful for Dad being here now. He spends a lot of time with Bud and knows how to make him feel better. During the first day or two of coming out of the operation Dad can spend his time with him entirely." With the use of sulfa drugs, which were new on the market and had to be flown in on a chartered plane from

Retirement

Canada, Bud gradually improved. As soon as he got out of the hospital, he and his mother and Susie flew to be with relatives in Southern California, where he recuperated for six months before returning home.

In 1948 Mr. Beck traveled to New York to preside over the wedding of another grandchild, Wayne's sister Joan. In the spring of 1949 his fourth granddaughter Susie graduated from high school and went on to college.

Then in 1951 his family circle increased when Bud married Mary Giraudo, a teacher from California, and they settled in Ketchikan to raise their family. Mr. Beck was 80 years old the first time Mary met him. Dressed in his best navy suit with tie and white shirt, he had gone down to the dock with the family to meet the Alaska Steamship Aleutian as the newlyweds disembarked in Ketchikan. Even at this first brief meeting Mary was won by his warm bright smile and felt a quiet power in his manner. Her love and admiration for this humble, great man grew with her acquaintance. When George Douglas was born in May of 1952 he became the fourth George Beck in the family living in Ketchikan. The original George Beck had died in 1939 in New York.

Mary and her children, first Doug and later Steve and Katy, delight in

George H., George J., and George L. (Bud) with George Douglas.

Retirement

their memories of being invited by their great grandfather to have chocolate with him at the Blue Fox whenever he met them in town. He came to their home for their birthdays and spent Christmas and other family holidays with the entire family. During social gatherings at the family home, he sat as a quiet, dignified presence. Often there were weddings for him to perform in the various churches and occasionally in the parlor at Marge and George's, which Marge would decorate appropriately for the event. Parties were given at the church on his birthday. Mrs. Royer, church organist, baked a cake for each birthday. She remembers seeing him pass her house on Sunday walking to church as she herself was getting ready. "When I arrived at church, he would be in his regular place and would nod and smile. I really missed him when he could no longer be there. He was always so good to my daughter Shelley. Whenever we stopped by to see him on our way home, he would bring out the basket of toys which were kept for the Beck children's visits for her to play with while we talked. I remember him as a courtly gentleman of the old school. I never thought of him as old until a few days before he died."

He was frequently invited to offer the dedication at high school graduation services. In 1961 his church building was sold and a new one built farther from center of town.

On May 19, 1959 Mr. Beck was given Sheldon Jackson College's first Christian Citizenship Award. Of his nomination for the award, Rolland Armstrong, president of the college, wrote:

> *You have seen the beginning of churches, and Sunday schools, the organization of youth groups. You have been a farsighted planner in working for the hydroelectric plant that is now part of Sheldon Jackson. Before ROTC was part of the educational pattern of education you organized a group of Sitka Training School students to drill and handle guns. You sailed the seas of southeast Alaska as a mariner for heaven. Beyond this your recognition as a spiritual giant brought ordination. Through this your ministry went out to weddings, baptisms, and the comfort at the side of the grave.*

In her biography of Reverend Beck for the Sheldon Jackson Christian Citizenship award, Genevieve Mayberry reported his feelings about being

Retirement

asked to give the prayer of dedication at the opening of the Ketchikan Pulp Mill in 1954.

> *One of the greatest thrills of his life came when he was asked to make the dedicatory prayer when the Ketchikan Pulp Mill was dedicated. The coming of this tremendous industrial plant to Southeastern Alaska seemed to Mr. Beck the fulfillment of all the visions he had had of industry in this great timbered land when he had arrived as a teacher of simple carpentry so many years before.*
>
> *This was the dream in the heart of the young missionary who had built the flume from Indian River to turn those primitive water wheels at the Sitka Training School. What a far cry from that simple machinery to this streamlined giant of modern industry!*
>
> *"And to think," he exclaimed, "that before they threw those tremendous switches, they asked the help of God Almighty! And the great honor that was mine in being the one asked to make the prayer!"*

As the years rolled by he became Ketchikan's Grand Old Man and was elected Citizen of the year. Then in 1961 he fell and broke his hip, and since

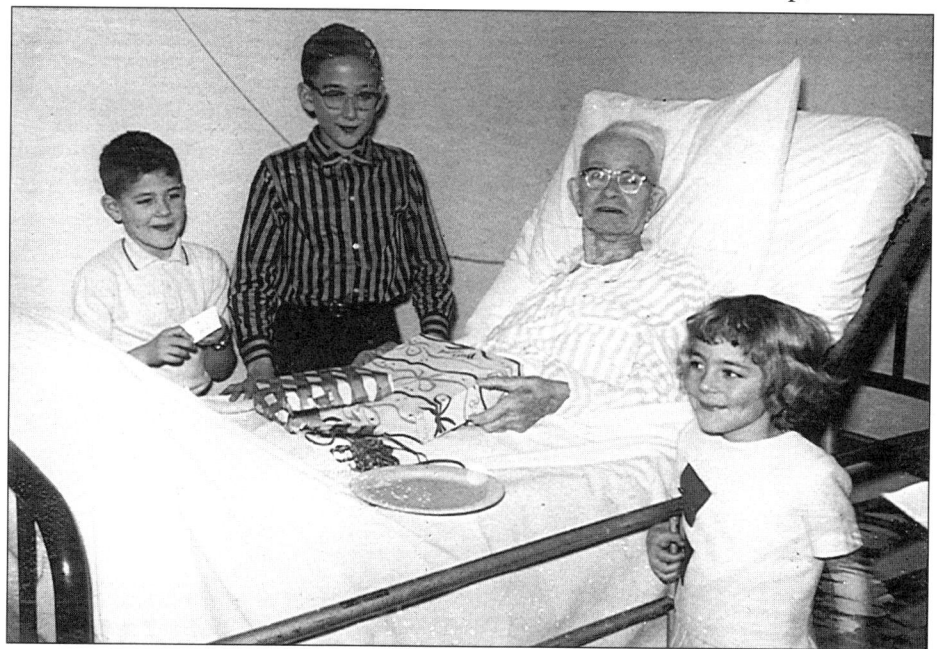

Children with Great Grandpa in the Hospital.

Retirement

there was no Pioneer Home in Ketchikan it looked as though he might have to go to Sitka. But the Sisters of St. Joseph at the local hospital, appreciative of his help in ministering to people there over the years, made it possible for him to stay near his family. They were able to put him in a room of a wing of the hospital that had been closed, where he received long term care for a more reasonable amount than hospital care would have been. Friends and relatives visited him daily and went away cheered by him. He always had a smile and a humorous story. Nurses and doctors stopped by for a pleasant chat. The grandchildren were allowed to visit him through the back door.

The family held a party for Grandpa at Christmas at the hospital and gave gifts to the Sisters and the fourteen nurses who took care of him throughout his stay there. On his ninety-first birthday, March 29, 1962, the family had a birthday party for him. The children came with the family and brought him gifts and helped him to open them. Friends dropped in throughout the day.

He remained in the hospital for almost two years until his death in February 5, 1963, just short of his ninety-second birthday. His funeral was held in the new Presbyterian church and he was buried in Ketchikan Cemetery near his beloved Harriet. The services were presided over by the Reverend Pritchard and attended by other members of the Presbyterian clergy of Southeast Alaska: the reverends Schwab, Hartness, and Bruhen and the Methodist minister, the Reverend David Fison. Many of the people he had worked with over the years had preceded him in death, as had many who were in his flock. But friends from the community attended the funeral and condolences came in from all over Alaska and the States. One letter the family cherished especially was from William S. Paul, the renowned lawyer and Tlingit leader and son of Mr. Beck's good friend and fellow missionary, Tillie Paul.

Dear friend George,

When I was last in Ketchikan, I spent about two hours with your father. He was glad to see me for he was very lonely. We spent the time talking about the past. I suppose I have had more contact with Reverend Beck than anybody else alive, except of course the intimate relation that a son would have. I remember when he arrived in

Retirement

in Sitka in 1895. My mother and he used to go to the "village" every Thursday to hold a meeting of the "New Covenant Legion." Mother left brother Louis and me home with orders to go to bed at 8 p.m. and we did—never one minute earlier or later. I was in your father's troop and one picture I have showed me carrying a flag. Reverend Beck and Doctor Bert Wilbur were about the same build and nearly the same age. They had fine times together. Your sister was given her Indian name Kosseyia by my mother. I remember when your father and mother were married and went off on the honeymoon—a small boat and away.

Maybe I should take time and put down my recollections. The New Covenant Legion was the forerunner of the Alaska Native Brotherhood. It really only changed its name The same men were in both. [William Paul was the second president of the Alaska Native Brotherhood, succeeding its first president Andrew Hope].

I persuaded your father to leave Hoonah and had to overcome his reluctance by arguing that Mrs. Beck should be near you during the last years of her life. Your dad could not answer that argument. Of course, I also dwelt on the need, and that so far as I could see, there was a schism developing which a new pastor could not prevent but he could. Then my wife and I later became his right and left arms as I led the choir and Mrs. Paul was the pianist. He used to come in on practice and sit in a pew and just enjoy himself as I drilled about 30 of our young people. We practiced three nights a week and thus kept some away temptation who otherwise had no place to go but a bar. I think one of our last cantatas was entitled "The Heavenly Host" and everybody saw the humor of it when we had our picture taken under that sign.

We loved him to the very last.

He was in that near-war when the two tribes at Sitka disputed about who had the right to use the Frog totem. It took my mother and a Mrs. Newman to persuade the Coho Tribe chief to forgive the wrong about which he was enraged. Mother cut short her vacation and returned to Sitka all the way from Ashland, Oregon. At last, the chief said to mother: "You don't know me but I know you. We have the same common ancestor, a man named Gux-nah-woo (that was about eight generations back) and for that reason I will give in to

Retirement

you." And so this woman did what the Governor (Brady) was unable to do. Peace was restored.

When I saw him last, I knew he would not live much longer. But he was looking forward to the fulfillment of his life of faith. He was beautiful. His departure was very much like that of my mother and so we shall not mourn him, for his time had come. We can remember the wonderful life of service.

Sincere regards to you and your beautiful wife from Mrs. Paul and me. We are not getting any younger either. I knocked on the door in the last of February but St. Peter sent me back. I feel well now. (Signed) William S. Paul

And so George James Beck went to his final rest after a life of service to his church and to the communities of Southeast where he had lived. "The eye can not see the wonders that he has been instrumental in bringing about," said Genevieve Mayberry in her short biography, "for who can measure the value of one soul shown the pathway to God, or the intangible worth of a hand reached out in help? Surely the Lord has used George Beck in many ways to manifest His wonders." George Beck explains it in five simple words: "I worked for the Lord."

And so he went on to that reward he had worked toward all his life and had come the closest of any man to achieving on earth, that peace that passeth understanding.

Bud Presenting Painting of George J. Beck to Sheldon Jackson College.

THAT ALASKA MISSIONARY
By S. Hall Young
From the Presbyterian Magazine September 1923

[S. Hall Young was the minister at the first Presbyterian mission and church in Wrangell and founded mission settlements throughout Southeast Alaska in the 1880's. Later he also established missions throughout Northern Alaskan. He authored many books, among them *The Klondike Clan*, *Hall Young of Alaska* and *Alaska Days with John Muir.*]

I write you a story of romance and adventure. My hero is a hero indeed, although he doesn't look or claim the part. Physically he is not of heroic mould or feature. Rather below than above medium stature, he is yet straight and well built, and of soldierly bearing. His shock of iron gray hair, which always will stand straight up, convinces you of his fifty years, although his fresh complexion and mobile face dispute the fact. His blue eyes smile constantly. His movements are quick and certain.

George J. Beck is a New Yorker. His father was an artist of no mean ability, living on a farm near the Connecticut line. He and his family were strictly—in these looser days we would say severely—religious. Sabbath keeping was an essential part of the Moral Law. The Bible in King James' version was all inspired and every letter sacred. Faith, consecration, self-denial—these were the laws of that Christian home. Being far away from a school-house, private tutors supplied the education of the children. Religion was the chief study—religion and daily labor.

So George grew up into manhood without college or seminary training. But he could farm or build a house or set up an engine or sail a boat. And, better than that, he could lead a prayer meeting, conduct a service, or win a soul to Christ. To the Women's' Executive Committee of the Presbyterian Board of Missions, as it was then, came this merry-eyed boy one day, asking to be sent anywhere, to do any kind of Christian work. This seemingly irresponsible young fellow, whose every sentence ended in a laugh—what could he do? So they offered to send him as mechanic and drill master to Sitka, Alaska. For this work they tendered the munificent salary of fifty dollars a month. They expected a refusal; they found instant acceptance. Thus Beck came to the Sitka Training School. That was in 1895.

S. Hall Young Article

He found an unending round of varied duties awaiting him. He was "general utility man" for the Institute with its twenty teachers and its one hundred and fifty Indian scholars. Most eastern youths would have been bludgeoned dumb by the multitude and the newness of the duties, but George was not that kind. He laughed, took off his coat, and pitched in. Was there a raft of logs to be sought among the islands, cut down, floated out at high tide and brought by sail and long sweeps into the harbor of Sitka? He marshaled the big boys, jollied them up and did it. Out yonder was a patch of ground that might be coaxed into a garden to grow the potatoes and vegetables needed by those hundred and seventy-five hungry mouths. He led his squad with mattocks, spades and hoes; and lo, a wonderful garden! Long ditches were needed to drain the ground and install a water system. Foundations for new houses were to be dug and pipe lines laid. Beck's pick and shovel squad must be organized and taught.

Then those slouchy, shuffly, loose-jointed boys, who had never tried to stand up straight, who couldn't look you in the eye and didn't know how to obey. Why a military company is what is needed. The good ladies at 156 Fifth Avenue, New York, are doubtful but Beck has his way. The surgeon at the school has experience and common sense and stands by him. Presently there are soldierly boys standing straight, marching proudly, and at their head two worthy young captains.

At the close of the war a young soldier, just returned from abroad, was standing in the door of the Presbyterian Building, New York. A Secretary of one of the Boards came up to him with outstretched hands. "By your complexion I would take you to be an Indian."

"I am," replied the soldier.

"From what tribe?"

"I am from Alaska."

"Ah," said the Doctor of Divinity, " I suppose you young natives are so grateful to Uncle Sam for his care of you that you rallied to fight his battles when called upon."

"No, I don't feel grateful to Uncle Sam. He has done very little for us. He has taken our fishing places and lands and has not given us protection or the rights of citizens in return."

"Then what induced you to enter the World War?"

"Well," replied the young man with a smile, "I am a Presbyterian. I was drilled as a soldier at the Sitka Training School. My captain taught me to be brave, to love freedom and fight for the oppressed. I volunteered to fight for the cause of humanity because Mr. Beck taught me to."

George Beck made himself indispensable. Was there a building to be erected, he must superintend it. Were there engines to be installed or machinery to be placed, he must direct the job. Is the school left without a superintendent, who but Beck can fill the place. In all emergencies the natural answer was, "Let George do it."

One of the most sensible things he did must not be neglected. When he arrived at Sitka it did not take him long to find and fall in love with an attractive young lady who had been a teacher there for two years. After one year's acquaintance they were married, and Mrs. Beck has proved herself a worthy comrade of her resourceful husband. She has the same brave, glad spirit, the same adaptability, the same unswerving Christian faith.

There is a story of Beck, which I almost hesitate to tell. The people in Alaska who know its truth are divided into two camps, those who sneer at him for a fool and those who worship him as a Christian hero. Two of Beck's "boys" were out hunting on the west shore of Chichagof Island. They saw particles of yellow metal gleaming from the bed of a little creek. Hunting farther they found pieces of quartz with veins of gold running through them and more nuggets in the stream. Putting these specimens in their hunting bag, they brought them to their beloved teacher and captain. The laws did not permit the natives to stake gold claims. Mr. Beck traveled the ten or so miles with his boys and staked the ground in his own name for them. He recorded the claims and searched for a buyer. [Actually he had Mr. Kelly, a teacher at the school stake the claim in his name.] The boys offered him a half interest in the claim; he would not take it. They urged it upon them. He still refused. The value of the claims waxed to wonderful proportions. Capitalists paid large sums for shares. Ed DeGroff, a storekeeper who grubstaked the boys to the extent of fifteen dollars, got a quarter interest in the mine and has realized a fortune on his investment. The two boys who discovered the mine and two of the teachers who helped them have enough banked to yield them independent incomes for life.

But George Beck, who with his family of three was living on seventy-five dollars a month took nothing. The men of Sitka, who all liked him, shouted, "You're a fool if you don't take it!" His fellow teachers and his ministerial friends urged him: "Think of your boy and your girl and their education. Think of the good you could do and the missions you could support." To all these he returned one answer: " I have asked the Lord and he told me not to take this money. I haven't earned it. If I should accept it the Indians would lose confidence in me. They would say that I love gold like the rest of the white men." And so Beck and his wife plod along on a salary barely sufficient to provide for them. When you speak to Beck about the fortune he despised and rejected, he laughs and says, "I got more out of that mine than any of the other fellows.". . .

In 1912 the ministers of the Presbytery of Alaska all insisted that Beck should be ordained and put in charge of a mission. So in the old Mother Church in Wrangell this man, whose only theological seminary has been the mountain colonnades and glacier transepts and forest pillars, was solemnly set aside by the Presbytery to the work of the Gospel ministry. He was sent to a Kake tribe with a dark and bloody history. The Friends had done some work there and a little progress had been made, but the medicine men freely plied their trade and a deep resentment against the whites burned into the breasts of the older people. They met the new minister with sullen and suspicious looks. The people lived in large community houses, fifty or sixty in one room. . . . "Old fashions" predominated.

George and his wife began to clean up. They projected a cooperative sawmill. The people were stimulated to build single family cottages and to cultivate gardens. A church and manse were built; sidewalks connected the village with the salmon cannery; a brass band and a fire company were organized; the young men were drilled as soldiers and the girls were taught gymnastic exercises. The people straightened up and learned self-respect. . . .In 1915, the Kake Mission, having been set squarely on its feet, Beck was sent to the larger tribe and mission of Hoonah on Chicagof Island. . . He improved the buildings, and then went from house to house of this large village, stimulating the people to clean up, to reform, to build better houses, and to send their children to school. . . . Some of his old "boys" from Sitka Training school rallied round him. The last of the medicine men cut their hair. Persecution for witchcraft was made a thing of the past. The church advanced in numbers and influence. A town council was organized and the best of the Hoonahs put in its seats. A brass band gathered

S. Hall Young Article

together and again the young men drilled as a company.

The Hoonah Mission was marching forward finely when the World War broke out. Of course, George Beck was tinder to the match. Soon he was established in the Y.M.C.A. Hut at Hoboken. Later he was attached to the U.S.Transport Mongolia and made nine round trips with this great liner. He was known as the "Rustling Chaplain." The boys loved him and imposed upon him. He organized entertainments, dramatic plays, all kinds of stunts for the amusement of the boys, and he talked to them and preached the sermon of a consecrated Christian life everyday. Conversions were constant. Admirals and generals became his companions and praised him.

After the war's close he thought of devoting the rest of his life to work in the forts of the United States. We discussed this question many times. "But Alaska needs you," I urged. "You know those Indians as few do. They love you and want you. Other men can look after the soldier boys; there are no others to look after your Thlingets." For several months he pondered and prayed. Then one morning he came into my office and said as soon as he saw me, "I'll go back."

One small mission was vacant, Klukwan, up the Chilcat River. To this isolated village went Mr. and Mrs. Beck. They were there less than a year and in that time they rejuvenated the mission, organized an Indian council, ordained more elders, converted more natives. Then Hoonah, his old charge, having become vacant, they were sent back there and he was again given control of the Lois, our mission boat. This beautiful little craft had undergone many trials and tribulations. Awkward and neglectful men had mishandled it; it had been sunk at one time and nearly wrecked at others, and presented a forlorn and discouraged appearance when George Beck again walked its decks.

His heart was sick at the condition of the boat. He had taken charge of the Lois in 1914, had painted her and repaired her engines again and again. He went to work once more and with the help of Mr. Waggoner and other experienced workmen put her in running order. Each year since, for at least six months, the Lois has wound in and out among the intricate passages of the Alexandrian Archipelago. Her parish is a tremendous one. Over fifty towns and villages, twice as many canneries, thirty or forty mines, and over a hundred fishing camps, demand the helpful ministration of the mission boat. Twenty-five established missions call for her. An organ

S. Hall Young Article

and hymn books are always carried aboard her and a moving picture machine with many films is ready for the instruction and entertainment of the natives.

There is no place in all the world where a mission boat has so much to do or can accomplish so much good. In 1920 Mr. Beck preached to over four thousand natives. There are some fifteen thousand people in the Archipelago. While most of the natives have heard the Gospel and there are missions in nearly all the tribes, there are many summer camps that have never been reached. Practically all of these natives scatter to the hunting and fishing grounds during the warmer months. Many white men's camps also are entirely without a preached Gospel unless a wandering evangelist visits them. The Lois is the only boat to convey the Gospel messengers from point to point throughout the Archipelago.

I had the privilege during August of 1921 of cruising upwards of six hundred miles on the Lois. Rev. Waggoner, one of the best navigators in all this region and a boat builder as well, was our captain. His son Ralph, a boy of fifteen, was deck hand and general purveyor. Mr. Beck was engineer, steward, and general manager of the expedition and of all the religious meetings. Mrs. Beck was our splendid cook and stewardess. We sailed from Juneau, stopping each night at some cannery, mine, camp or town. We held meetings everywhere. We found the fishermen in their tents and boats and their families in their temporary houses. We visited the sick, counseled the inquiring ones and the wayward. I never made a trip anywhere that was better appreciated or fruitful of more results.

During the winter months Beck must remain as pastor at Hoonah. He has made this the most united, homogeneous, and progressive mission in Alaska. There are nearly two hundred members. The people are all Christians and all Presbyterian. It has been hard to get the natives of Alaska to give anything toward the support of their pastors or for the Boards. In the spring of 1921 Beck showed them the budget system and told them the needs of the Presbyterian Church. Then he sat back and let the officers and members talk. Soon they stopped talking and began to act. They took up a collection for the Board of Missions for $60. Then they discussed the budget for the next fiscal year and $200 was pledged towards the pastor's salary and more for incidentals and repairs, and every body was happy.

That is the way Beck manages.